# BRAVING

The Art of Pursuing What Makes You Come Alive

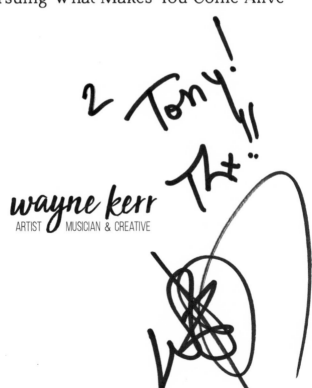

**wayne kerr**
ARTIST MUSICIAN & CREATIVE

*dedication*

This book is dedicated to my sweet family. You three have the keys to my heart. To my wife Kelley. You teach me daily what it means not only to be brave, but how to selflessly love others. Thank you for relentlessly supporting all my crazy endeavors.

To my two amazing daughters, Elliott and Emory. You already know this because I tell you every day, but I'll say it again. You two can do anything you want to with your lives. Put God first, and go for it. Go be brave, my loves.

Thank you to my bigger family, Terri & Dave, JoJo and Gary, Bruce and Doris, and all of the Kennedys! Thank you to my Grace Family for your love and support.

# acknowledgments

Thank you to Allen Arnold for helping steer this crazy dream/mission of mine into what BRAVING has become. I so appreciate your heart, insight and direction.

Thank you Virginia Bhashkar and Natalie Hanemann for the mad editing skills! You had to endure all of my added exclamation points and overuse of the words "awesome" and "super." Thank you for the hard work to pull the best out of my feeble attempts. Thank you, Lorie DeWorken, for typesetting the book. It's beautiful!

Thank you to all of the incredible and humble individuals who allowed me to meet with them and have these conversations—many of which are included in these pages, and many are not. All of you have blessed me and taught me so much.

Lastly, thank you to you the reader. I am fully aware that in a busy world with much noise, it truly is a complete blessing that you would pause long enough to read what I have to share here. Thank you!

# friends

A special thank you to these amazing folks who pre-ordered this book long before it was even done. Thank you so much for encouraging me, and believing in this project. I pray that you are inspired big time to keep Braving!

Parker Battle, Shelly Miller, Laura McLean, Nathan O'Grady, Enrico Castagnetti, Dana Stoerkel, Bill Parker, Christine Norwood, Cathie Woitena, Debbie Robb, Gale Freed, Shannon Stubblefield, Jon Hendricks, Jerry Heinold, Nan Masterson, Nolan Burke, Tara Royer Steele, Kevin Gilmore, Shara Mckinley, David Rudd, Sharlette Ream, Terri Dietrich, Barbara Francis Yehl, Brian Heard, Roni Allen, Kent Stuckey, Wendy Toups, Julie Craig, Debbie Henderson, Mindy Williams, David Michael Hyde, Donna Newell, Brad Knippenberg, Titi Dayas Barry, Cheryl Poese, Jim Leggett, K Kallus, Kerri Perkins, Rudolf Gaulke, Lori Lien, Andy Hong, Dara Bell, Karen Danford, Beau and Kelly Brotherton, Dave Veach, Shane Elson, Catherine Eaton, James Hornstra, Kay Schneider, Sandra Roberson, Renee Battle, Eric Glass, Jan Whitehead, Neva Kerr, Lori Kluesner, Suzanne Sexton, Nate Shallenberger, Ashley Bendickson, Patsy Scoggins, Cathy Marshall, AJ Bass, Bonnie Azadan, Stephanie Darmer, Linda Delerme, Barbara Metzler, Jennifer McCarroll, Brian K Smith, Kip and Wendy Thomson, Shaan Tippett, Jordan Herrera, Devin Holmes, Rhonda Laughlin, Paul Trone, Lacey Wolan, Connie Jo Carter, Maggie Cruz, Eme Abu, Linda Bohn, Sylvia Moreau, Evelyn Martin, Nancy Simmons, Debbie Carroll, Ruth Dodd, Leslie Power, Will Drescher, Shelley Weaver, Sam DeFranco, Allison Corgey, Karen Overleese, JoAnn Kerr, Prasanna Victor Prasad, Susan Hall, Keomi Martin, Chantal Johnson, Silas and Nancy Borden, Inita Sampay, David Smith, Liz Allen, Penny Miner, Olen Gandy, Susan Kicey, Maria Connor, Melissa Garza, Achim Meissner, Susy McAdams, Jennifer Schmidt, Ashley Dubois, Naoko Tonaki, Ron and Cher Hayes, Harrison Hart, Helen Martin, Heather Keahey, Deb Smith, Leigh Ann Schweser, Tiffany Cobb, Michelle Perozo, Haley Sebree, Ellen Kirkland, Leah Gaffney, Mindy Keahey, Scooter Lofton, Maegen Lane, Kyra Lynne Bussing, Jamie Bruning, Stephanie Kistler, Benjamin Yeu Chai

# contents

# A TREEHOUSE

> Don't ask yourself what the world needs. Ask yourself what makes you come alive, and then go do that. Because what the world needs is people who have come alive.
>
> —Howard Thurman

A treehouse. That is what Kelley, my sweet wife of eighteen years, requested for her most recent birthday. I knew the idea was partially inspired by our two little girls, Elliott and Emory, who are seven and five years old, but a treehouse fits right along with Kelley's adventurous spirit. She loves being outdoors in nature, and more importantly, she loves being with people. A treehouse big enough to hold a gathering invites both. We have a few acres of land in South Central Texas where we just love to go, and this would be the perfect addition out there.

*I got this*, I thought. I would be brave and build the treehouse with my bare hands! If I could pull this off it would be epic—it would truly bless my sweetheart and be a great source of memories for years to come. Plus, I could have bragging rights for ages!

Now, I knew absolutely nothing, zippo, nada about construction. But I felt excited by the prospect of trying to tackle something that was completely unknown to me. How hard could it really be? It wasn't like I was going to build a house or do a full-scale Chip and Jo remodel or something. I was thinking more along the lines of a platform, raised eight to ten feet in the air, bolted into two oak trees.

Then came the little whispers: "You'll probably screw this up," and "Just wait till those guys at the lumberyard see your clueless face." In all honestly, I *did not* want my girls and their friends, not to mention my lovely wife and her friends, to fall out of this thing I was about to construct. *D'oh!*

1

I've learned from the remarkable author and counselor John Eldredge a thing or two about the concept of "making agreements."[1] Basically, when you hear negative voices, either in your own head or coming from other people, and you say, "Yep, that's right. I agree. I'll mess this up for sure," you're making an agreement to do that very thing.

For me, it's almost a doggone daily struggle just deciding *not* to make agreements with negative voices. They're sneaky, I tell you, and they can honestly break me down or stop me in my tracks before I even take one baby step. Thankfully, I know myself well enough to notice when I start making agreements, so I try to be ready to press on in the presence of doubt.

I wanted to do this thing! I would tackle the treehouse head on.

I know it's just a treehouse, and my struggle may even seem a bit silly, but I believe that moving toward the thing we don't know much about, whatever it may be, or pushing ourselves beyond what's safe and familiar, is a huge test for our hearts. It's what I call "braving."

It can be frightening.

It can be awesome!

We are rewarded.

Off I went, drawing up some plans on my handy yellow notebook paper. As you might imagine, hilarity soon followed. My first sketches looked great. *Hey, I got this*, I thought. Then I actually started Googling "Build your own treehouse."

I quickly realized I had no idea what the following things were:

- Carriage bolt
- Lag screw
- Ledger
- Joist
- Galvanized screws and fasteners (versus regular)
- Header
- Dovetail

*Dovetail?* Okay, I needed to call for backup.

I called my friend Andy Crawley. Andy knows construction. Andy knows concrete. Andy also plays drums—really well. He toured for over a decade with

Chris Tomlin and has played with tons of amazing people. But what I love about Andy is that he's not defined only by that season in his life. He loves God and loves his family, and on top of knowing he's a great guy, I knew he would be merciful. I texted him some pictures of my little drawings, with a message that simply read, "Help!"

Andy called me, ready to save the day. "We can make this work," he said. "Let me ask you, do you have a post hole digger?"

"No."

"I have one you can borrow. Do you have a circular saw?"

"No."

"No worries, I have one of those, too. Do you have a power drill and socket and ratchet set?"

"Ha. No! I have a battery-powered screwdriver." I could feel things deteriorating quickly.

"Do you have a tape measure?" Andy asked.

"Yes, I have that!" (I could keep my Man Card, I think.)

It's true that we all have our areas of expertise. For most of my adult life, I've been a songwriter and touring musician. I spent sixteen years on the road doing about 180–200 events per year. I recorded nine albums during that time, and I even had a song reach number sixty-three on the pop charts in the Netherlands, where it stayed for one week. Ha! So, if you ask me musical stuff, like why certain chord progressions seem familiar to all of us or how much compression to use on your bus mix, I could talk all day. Or, since my college degree was in visual art, we could easily discuss painting, drawing, and sculpture techniques, and I would get lost in the chatter.

I'm sure you know exactly what I mean. You probably have an area or two (or five) where you feel quite in your element. Maybe you've worked in the same field for over twenty years and you know it inside and out. Maybe you are just finishing up your degree in a certain subject, and with so much fresh knowledge about it, you're safely in your wheelhouse. With your eyes closed, and one hand tied behind your back, you could teach me more about it than I could imagine.

Well, my friend, for each of us there is always something new to learn. Something that could awaken part of our hearts that we didn't even know was asleep. Believe me, I wasn't thinking about this growth prospect as I made my first trip of many to the lumberyard. Before this thing was all said and done, I graced the doors of Lowes, Home Depot (several times), McCoy's Building Supply (like, four times), and even Tractor Supply Co. In and out of their doors I went, uncovering and braving so many funny learning curves along the way.

After finalizing the plans for the treehouse, I counted and re-counted what I was about to order from the lumberyard. I also figured I better order a bit extra in case I screwed something up along the way.

The day finally came for the large load of lumber to be delivered out at our land. Early that morning, I met the driver at the cattle gate that sits at the end of a long, dirt county road. He followed me through another cattle gate and onto our property. The gravel road disappeared, and we began driving on grass, honking to get the cows out of the way. We arrived at the area where our new treehouse was destined to become a reality. I parked and pointed to where we would unload.

This process alone was like my official induction to the beginning of a huge learning curve. I grabbed my work gloves and looked at the large load of wood on the back of a flatbed delivery truck. I thought to myself, *I'm about to get my workout for the day unloading this stuff!* On the bed of the truck I saw the huge, two-by-ten-by-fourteen-foot beams I would be using. There were also some sixteen-foot-long posts and they sure seemed ginormous. I saw stacks upon stacks of lumber in the various sizes I'd ordered and thought, *This is actually awesome.*

I stretched my back a few times and moved my shoulders a bit to loosen up. I guessed that at minimum it would take the delivery guy and me about thirty minutes to unload. I Velcro'd tight my gloves and turned my hat backward. *Let's do this!* Ever the valiant warrior, I was crossing into uncharted lands for the one I love.

That's when he did it.

The delivery guy hit a button on his truck, and the entire truck bed lifted into the air. I stood there, somewhat shocked, as it slowly went higher and higher. About thirty seconds later, I watched as my entire delivery slid onto the ground. Then the driver pulled his truck forward and hit the button again, sending the truck bed back to its regular position, before simply saying, "Sign here."

I took my gloves off—I tried to do it without him seeing—and within two minutes he had driven out of sight, as I stood there thinking, *Oh. Yeah. I totally knew we were going to do it like that.*

That's when I knew that class had begun, and I strongly suspected I'd be learning lots by trial and error.

Over the next three weekends, this project unfolded. Several friends and neighbors were kind and gracious enough to help in the process. Still, before I reached the finish line I would:

- Hang one of the beams upside down, messing up the pre-cut measurement I'd made
- Fall off a ladder
- Hammer a carriage bolt, instantly messing up the threading so the nut wouldn't fit
- Stretch the very limits of patience in my dear wife and children; bless them, Lord
- Measure correctly, and cut incorrectly
- Call Andy
- Drive a power drill into my finger
- Measure incorrectly, and cut correctly
- Somehow miscount how many screws would be needed, again
- Go back to the hardware store
- Call Andy, again
- Run out of concrete mix twice, somehow
- Some other stuff I can't even remember

At one point, as I started placing the joist beams across the top of the treehouse, Kelley said, "It doesn't really look level."

"It's totally level," I said.

Then our neighbor Leon drove up in his truck with his young grandson. Leon said, "Nope, doesn't really look level. That was the first thing my grandson said as we drove up, 'Grandpa, that doesn't look very level.'"

I measured and looked again, and guess what? I was only off on one end of the floor by three and a half inches. A discrepancy which, in fact, means that your floor is not level. Not even close, y'all.

Three weeks later, despite all of these trials, the Kerr treehouse was finally completed. Somehow, by God's good graces, this thing was finished, and I had lived to tell the tale.

That night, we ate our dinner ten feet up in the canopy of our oak trees, as the breeze blew and the golden hour of late afternoon began. I watched my little girls pull the rope we'd attached to an old rusty pulley, which we'd taken from my father-in-law's cabin in the mountains of New Mexico, and hoist up a bucket full of their stuffed animals. And we hung the American flag up high in the treehouse.

I sat back and watched Kelley enjoy her birthday gift and laugh with our daughters. I couldn't help but imagine the memories that lie ahead in this very space. It was a wild and beautiful moment. I found myself wishing my dad was alive to see it; honestly, he wouldn't believe it. Mainly because for the fact that I had actually used power tools to build something like this. I knew he would be beaming.

I looked over at the dried handprints of our two girls in the concrete at the base of the ladder, and I thought, *Wow. What a blessing. Thank you, God. I am blessed beyond measure.*

I learned a lot, and I realized I want to keep learning and growing. I want to be stretched in the process that takes me from shrinking in fear to feeling more alive than ever. I powered through my need to act like I knew all the answers. I've *still* got a lot to learn, and I want to live life by braving it. I'm okay with taking on the unknown because I've experienced the reward of doing just that.

Can I ask you a question? What is your treehouse? What is the thing you are hoping to build? It may not involve wood or nuts and bolts. What dream are you considering jumping into with both feet? What makes your heart fully come alive?

Whatever it is that makes your heart come alive, I encourage you to pursue it. I want to help you experience the rewards of braving your life.

But first, I need to go return all these tools to Andy!

*introduction*

# THE MAKING OF *BRAVING*

"You will have to do without pocket handkerchiefs, and a great many other things, Bilbo Baggins, before we reach our journey's end. You were born to the rolling hills and little rivers of the Shire, but home is now behind you, the world is ahead."[2]

—*The Hobbit: An Unexpected Journey*

Last year I turned fifty. *What?!* It was fairly traumatic for me, but age is just a number—right?

If you're younger than me, you may think that fifty is old (this is for sure what I thought when I was younger). If you're older than fifty, you may think, *Get over it, dude, you're still young!* Still, I have to say, turning fifty started to seem like a bigger deal to me the closer it got to my birthday.

I suddenly realized that my forties were coming to an end. I was startled to be coming up on half a century—*half a century!* I called my mom and asked, "Can you believe that fifty years ago, you had me as a baby? Wow, I am old, Mom!" (I was also sure to mention to my mom that she is amazing and still rocking it at eighty-four.)

Like most people who cross this threshold, I sensed it was a good time for me to stop and evaluate the past as well as the future. And at least I happened to be presented with the perfect opportunity to be doing this. I had been given a sabbatical from my worship leader position and was literally going to be able to take a two- to three-month break after having served for more than seven years. At no point in my life had I ever had such a blessing. I knew it would be a true gift to be able to hit the pause button like that.

Guilt quickly tried to work its crafty way into my heart as my break got closer. I had thoughts like, *There are so many other people who deserve a break like this, and they're not you. You know who should've gotten a sabbatical? Your dad, your mom, and your sister.* Once again, I had to decide to squash those negative thoughts and just receive the gift.

I reminded myself that I had been going at full speed for basically all of my adult life. I had worked in graphic design for three years right out of college. Then, I had stepped out in faith into full-time music ministry, and that had turned into sixteen years on the road. As anyone who knows a full-time musician most likely knows, you have to be out playing live to make ends meet. I'm beyond grateful for that season in my life, when I often had the chance to sing in front of thousands—or even tens of thousands—of folks from across the country and abroad. I had been able to experience things that I never dreamed possible, even performing in places like Japan, Singapore, and other incredible countries, while selling more than 100,000 albums. For an independent artist, that meant I was successful and staying busy.

Then, eight years ago, I took a position with my home church leading worship, while still doing some traveling for music. Soon after, my wife and I welcomed our amazing little girl, Elliott, and then we welcomed our second, Emory, and life continued to remain crazy busy. We were juggling work, parenting, ministry, and I had a budding art career, too; it was a lot. My sabbatical "pause" was coming at the perfect time, and I could sense that my heart needed it big time.

To be completely honest, I had been asking myself some huge questions about my work life anyway. Something had been stirring in my heart, nudging me to step back into more of my artwork and creative life. Why was I feeling unsettled? Who in the world considers a career change at fifty? As a person of extreme faith who tries to walk daily with God, I even asked myself whether making a change in my church job position would be the same as bailing on my calling. I wondered, *Am I being selfish for wanting to listen to my heart?*

So, yeah, this break was clearly coming at a pivotal moment in my life. I would use it to think through this major life milestone—turning fifty—as well as the career changes my heart was longing to explore.

One of the things that I wanted to do during my sabbatical was to reach out to different people who have inspired me over the years. I wanted to see if they'd be open to grabbing coffee or having a phone or Zoom chat. I began reaching out to musicians who I've looked up to, painters, artists, filmmakers, and other creatives, as well as entrepreneurs and faith leaders. Some were actually quite well-known within their circles, and some were not in the public eye at all.

Many were open to the idea, and while some were not, I started getting really excited about the interviews I had managed to line up. I wanted to pick some peoples' brains about so many things that I'd been processing. I wanted to find out what made these people tick. I wanted to learn from them, and to learn from their stories. I had questions, y'all!

In my discussions with people who were successful in their respective industries, I asked questions like: "How do you get past obstacles and doubt?" "What would you tell your younger self?" "How has your faith kept you grounded in your life?" "What have been some of your greatest ups and downs?" Teach me, Obi-Wan!

As I started connecting with these amazing people, it soon became clear to me that this whole thing was awesome. It was unreal to be able to just sit down for an hour with someone and talk, especially because each person is someone I truly admire. Each time I left a meeting, I would sit awestruck in my truck and say, "Wow, that was incredible!" Then I would take to my journal and record the main points of my conversations.

With each conversation, I learned a huge truth or a giant life lesson, or I gained a nugget of inspiration that blew me away. And I began to realize that other people needed to hear all of this.

*Braving* is a project that started off with conversations and writings that were meant just for me. But, in the process, I came to believe it could be a *huge* inspiration to others. Why would I want to keep this wisdom and encouragement to myself? I knew I had to share it, and so I determined to write this book.

As the list of folks I talked to started growing, the concept morphed into fifty epic interviews with fifty epic people in my fiftieth year. (In fact, *Epic 50* was the original working title of this book you are reading.)

But as the conversations continued, I started to notice a stronger common thread in them. I realized that no matter their profession or passion, everyone I spoke with was navigating their journey in their own powerful way. They were facing down their fears and boldly pursuing their destinies. They were taking the chances that needed to be taken to live their callings.

No artist is immune from having to face a blank canvas again. No songwriter is immune from sitting at a piano in silence wondering how the song should be written. No one is immune from the voices of doubt I mentioned earlier, not to mention the voices of naysayers out there. To step into the unknown is a risky thing. It's called the unknown for a reason. But doing so is what braving is all about. That's what the people I spoke with are doing, and that's what I want to be doing on a regular basis. I encourage you to do so as well, and I hope this book will help.

If you are like me, you face obstacles and have doubts and questions. Even on the day that I decided to move forward with writing this book, I started hearing the voices of doubt: *Who am I to write a book? What in the world am I doing? You do know that no one will actually read this, right, or for that matter, care? So you are the authority on "braving" now, eh?*

Any of this seem familiar to anyone else? These are the thoughts that have been raging against me for weeks as I've prepared to start this process of typing out over a year's worth of chats and interviews. If you'll notice, some of this "inner voice" business was apparently coming from myself, my own insecurities. But interestingly enough, some of the thoughts in my head were directed to me as "you." Wait a second, who was saying these things? Where was this voice coming from?

I shared these inner doubts with my sister Terri, and she had a spot on response. "It sounds to me like you are getting a chance to walk out the very things you are writing about." Whoa. Wait a second, she was totally on target. I didn't want to hear that, but she was right. But even so, wow, as a writer, staring at a blank "page one" on the screen is ridiculously intimidating.

Well, my friend, we are not alone in this braving thing. People who have had massive success in business often pause and fret over their next move. Someone who wrote a hit song three years ago still has to bravely climb the Everest of a new unwritten piece.

As I started compiling the content of this book, I saw a pattern. Nine important lessons came to the surface. They became the focus of the nine chapters in *Braving*, titled: "Be You—There's Only One"; "See Your Life as a Story";

"Defeat the Doubt and Jump"; "Meraki"; "Get Good at Failing"; "Significance versus Success"; "Be Present, Be Thankful"; "Be a Lifelong Learner"; and "Get to Know the Storyteller."

In the pages that follow, you'll get to see the positive impact of these lessons on my life, and hopefully, you'll begin to apply them to your own. Within each chapter, you'll see snippets from the best and most powerful interviews I had. I'll also share stories from my own journey, along with questions for you to ponder at the end of each section.

You'll notice that many of the discussions I had involve faith. These were particularly meaningful to me personally. As a believer in God and follower of Christ, my faith plays a huge role in my daily decision-making and life. Wherever you are on your own life and spiritual journey, I pray you'll be encouraged by these open conversations and the truth they reveal about life, perseverance, and calling. I believe you will benefit in huge ways, as I have, from sitting in on these discussions.

And let's be honest, the people in my life who are truly braving it are those who are tackling illness head on, raising kids as single parents, or even walking into burning buildings to put out the fires. There are levels of brave, that's for sure. What I do know is this: When it's *your* turn to have to be brave, in whatever arena, the challenges are real, and the voices saying you should go ahead and quit are real. Is it possible to not believe the negative voices, to move past them, and to do the thing you long to do? Be the person you long to be? Here's what I do know, there is only one you, and the world desperately needs you to be you!

One day, if my two little girls read this, I pray they will be encouraged and be braving whatever comes their way. I tell them basically every day, "You can be whatever you want to be in this life. Put God first and you can be and do anything you can imagine! Go for it, girls!"

That goes for you, too.

*Braving* is the art of pursuing what makes you come alive. My friend, you're standing on the edge, mustering the courage to take the first step. The fact that you are holding this book right at this moment is, I believe, a divine appointment for you. Anyone who is reading a book called *Braving* is either believing enough to pursue a dream they've long had on the back burner, or is facing headfirst into a storm that has come their way. Whatever the case may be, I pray that within the pages that follow you will find serious nuggets of truth, encouragement, and tools to help you on your way.

I am no expert on anything, and I'll say that up front. But the experience of writing this book over the last year has been mind-blowing for me, and I am honored to share what I have learned with you here. Thank you for being brave enough take this journey with me.

So, grab your backpack, your hiking shoes, and let's do this.

Onward.

"To live would be an awfully big adventure."[3]

—*Peter Pan*

## *chapter one*

# BE YOU—THERE'S ONLY ONE

**braving.**

VERB (USED WITH OBJECT)

To meet or face courageously:

To defy; challenge; dare.

To make splendid [4]

I would like to add to this definition the following: "The art of pursuing what makes you come alive."

Over the years of full-time traveling and doing music, many of my events were at youth retreats and camps. One of my favorite topics to share with the attendees was about us being God's masterpiece, based on the Bible verse Ephesians 2:10: "For we are God's masterpiece. He has created us anew in Christ Jesus, so we can do the good things he planned for us long ago" (NLT).

As I'd urge students to contemplate just how very special they each were and what it means to be God's masterpiece, I often challenged them to do something, and I'll ask you to do it now, too. Look at your fingertip. I mean closely—look at it! Notice the many curved lines and pattern all its own?

May I remind you of a few crazy facts? No two identical sets of fingerprints have ever been recorded, not even among twins or triplets who can share the same DNA patterns.[5] When you were a baby in your mother's womb, at twenty-three weeks or so along, the patterns of your fingertips were complete. And koala bears have them, too![6] But that's another book.

There's only one you. Let that sink in. You are the only you God made, with special characteristics and unique gifts. Even when you face doubt or opposition, or when it seems easier to blend in than to stand out, please be you; we need you!

So many of the people I interviewed for *Braving* believe that it's best for people to be themselves, and I share this view. As a musician, if I try to copy another musical artist exactly, it might work for a second, just because of trends. But even if I nail it, I'm just a copy, and the audience is already moving on to the next trend. (And I'll most likely be sued.) If I copy another painter or illustrator exactly, guess what? It might improve my skills by offering opportunity for practice, but all I'll be is a copycat.

For the computer geeks out there, I have something for you. Look at the symbols below. I have an amazing T-shirt that simply has this printed on it. Do you know what it means?

$$\mathcal{H}N > \mathcal{H}C$$

It means Command New is greater than Command Copy. Translation: New is better than a copy. Way better.

It's my hope and prayer that as you read these fun and inspiring interviews, you're encouraged to be yourself. The people I had conversations with are not trying to be anyone else. For whatever reason, they gave up on that years ago. They are allowing themselves to be themselves; they are pursuing what makes them come alive, and the world is better for it. I hope that you will own your identity—not 60 percent, not 82 percent, but completely. I believe God created you with and for a grand purpose. No one else on this planet has your fingertips. In fact, no one who has ever lived does!

There is only one you.

# BEN MASTERS

> "I have this amazing idea. We need to make it a law that all members of Congress have to spend two weeks of the year together on a canoe trip in our national public lands. This would solve a ton of our problems. Spending a couple weeks with someone out on the river to work hard together, eat together, and look each other in the eye— it would do wonders. They'd see themselves and each other against the backdrop of the Grand Canyon, and yeah, they'd get some real perspective. When you get right down to it, we're all the same."

Speaking of someone who embodies what it means to be himself, one of the first guys I reached out to during this adventure was Ben Masters. Ben is a wildlife advocate, filmmaker, writer, and photographer. He has written for *National Geographic* and *Western Horseman* as well as two books of his own. He's received several awards, including the audience-chosen awards from international film festivals Telluride Mountain Film Festival, Banff Mountain Film Festival, and more. He's also the recipient of the South by Southwest (SXSW) Louis Black Lone Star Award. Ben makes visually stunning and powerful movies about wildlife and wildlife habitats.

My introduction to Ben's work was the documentary *Unbranded*. In this film Ben and several college friends shed light on the state of the wild mustangs in America. The documentary shows them hand-selecting fifteen wild horses from captivity, then spending three months breaking and training them. They then embarked on a four-month journey riding horseback all the way from the Mexican border to the Canadian border. Wild!

If you have not seen this film, do yourself a huge favor and go see it. I've watched it five times. The first time I saw it, I bounced back and forth between thoughts like, *This is so amazing!* to *These guys might actually die right now!* There's a scene in which Ben is fly fishing in the middle of a river somewhere in Montana, when a huge storm rolls in. Lightning is flashing and the rain is pounding, but he is so in the moment that there is no way he is going to miss it. He keeps right on fishing and yelling with this huge smile on his face. *Unbranded* is an exciting film that nobody could watch without being stirred to adventure.

In another powerful scene, a mustang loses its footing and tumbles downhill. Scary stuff. The horse was okay, but the real risk involved in making this documentary is captured. Ben is passionate about the wild lands in our nation and passionate about the wildlife that lives there. Because I was so moved by his work, I knew I had to reach out to Ben.

One of the things that first connected us was art. I did a painting showing Ben on horseback leading a few pack horses behind him—a scene from his film. I reached out to him and said I wanted to give him the painting as a gift. It's maybe a bit odd and somewhat risky, I know, to offer art to someone. (But as you'll see later in this book, it's been a great connecter for me with a few people.) He was blown away by the painting and was thrilled to meet up. We decided to meet in Austin, Texas at the one and only Cosmic Coffee.

What I'm about to reveal about that meeting is a low moment in my journey of manhood. When Ben and I stepped up to order a coffee before heading outside to chat, Ben ordered "a cup of coffee, black." And I, not being much of a coffee guy, ordered a café mocha because at least I knew it would have some sweet stuff in it. Well, to my horror and dismay, the barista at the counter handed Ben his coffee in a regular coffee cup, while my mocha arrived in an obnoxiously huge mug on a saucer. To make matters worse, it had that little "heart" shape in the top of the milk foam!

Ben said with a smile, "Wow, look at that."

This guy had ridden wild horses across the entire country, and on our first meeting I had ordered a freaking heart-decorated bowl of coffee on a saucer! I quickly hefted up that mug, leaving the saucer on the counter, and took a few fast sips to make the heart disappear. *Geez!*

Thank goodness that at least Ben loved the painting I brought him. We discussed it, along with other topics, at our visit.

BEN: Those horses here in the painting are Violet and Dinosaur. They are both amazing. Thank you for this painting, man. Wow, I don't know what to say.

WAYNE: Man, you are using your art through film and writing to connect to people. I am just doing the same thing. I appreciated the film so much—super inspiring! Thanks so much for taking the time to chat. So, how in the world did you get into all of this?

BEN: Well, it's obvious that there's nothing more important in the universe than wildlife. It's obvious! *[laughing]* I grew up in Texas around horses, and not too far from the ranch life. The outdoors has always been a part of my life. I went to Texas A&M to study wildlife biology; it just seemed like a perfect fit for me.

WAYNE: Tell me how the *Unbranded* film idea came to be.

BEN: Basically, my friends and I were graduating college and all had this same fear. That we would graduate, get a boring job that none of us really loved, make seventy thousand a year, and then be stuck there. A lot of people unfortunately get trapped and can't get out. We knew we had to do this crazy thing. We had done some smaller trips with wild mustangs, but nothing like this. I just knew we had to capture it on film.

The film *Unbranded* launched Ben into other film projects including *The River and the Wall, Deep in the Heart: A Texas Wildlife Story,* and more. In our conversation, his passion for the outdoors and his love for sharing the wild with other people was obvious. He gave me tips about places to see when I'm in Colorado. He shared how people complain about all sorts of things he has worked on. I guess it's the nature of the beast. But what here's what I found to be one of the best things he said that day . . .

BEN: I have this amazing idea. We need to make it a law that all members of Congress have to spend two weeks of the year together on a canoe trip in our national public lands. This would solve a ton of our problems. Spending a couple weeks with someone out on the river to work hard together, eat together, and look each other in the eye—it would do wonders. They'd see themselves and each other against the backdrop of the Grand Canyon, and yeah, they'd get some real perspective.

WAYNE: Genius. Let's vote that into law. You are obviously passionate about your work, bro. I can clearly see it in your films; you are fully alive out there. Any idea of why more people don't pursue what makes them come alive?

BEN: I think most people have that one thing that they are passionate about, and they wish they could either spend more time on it or do it for a living. I know that in many cases circumstances just prohibit it, you know? I'm very lucky and thankful. I just know, for me, it comes down to this: I just can't imagine myself not pursuing what I'm passionate about—our wild lands, the wildlife that lives there, and how to preserve it.

WAYNE: Okay, my last question: You are thirty-one, right? What would thirty-one-year-old Ben Masters tell twenty-year-old Ben Masters?

He sat in silence. Then he sat some more. I honestly appreciated the fact that he pondered this question for several moments before answering.

BEN: Budget your time, like you do your money. It's just as important, if not more.

Such a powerful time with this guy. A big takeaway for me: Be true to the real you. I can't see Ben sitting all day in a cubical on the twelfth floor of some building every day. Can you? While it works for some, it wouldn't be the right fit for him. The amazing byproduct of Ben being true to his heartbeat is that, by doing what he loves, he is inspiring thousands of people to get outside. Perhaps Ben's example of spending time in Creation, deeply breathing the air out in our wild lands, will encourage you to get outside, go to a state park, or go for a hike. Amidst the sounds of nature, with a silenced phone, perhaps you'll consider what it is that refreshes your own heart. What is it that makes you come alive; how can you impact your world by pursuing your unique calling.

And remember, if you go grab coffee with an epic cowboy-filmmaker-adventurer-conservationist, just go ahead and order whatever you want. It's cool.

Check out more about Ben (and all the folks I interviewed) in the resource list located at the end of this book.

## MARK MAGGIORI

> "People sometimes ask me, 'Do you get tired of painting horses and cowboys?' And I'm like, 'No way!' I think there's an element, too, that being from France, the American spirit is so powerful, and the people that ventured out into these wild lands to make a life for themselves are so inspiring."

One artist blazing his own path and boldly pursuing his unique calling is Mark Maggiori. Mark is a western art painter who was born in France and is now based in Los Angeles, and who is soon to be relocating to Taos, New Mexico. At forty-two, Mark has taken the western art world by storm. His paintings are stunning, featuring huge western clouds, cowboys on horseback, and massive canyons. His most recent works have auctioned off for tens of thousands of dollars. This guy's work is amazing.

I wanted to pick his brain about not only art, but music, too. He was part of a successful rock band in France for over a decade and then turned to his art. Both music and art being parts of my story, I couldn't wait to hear his. Plus, he has a super cool French accent. I had the pleasure of speaking with him over the phone.

WAYNE: Did you do art as a kid? What age did you start taking it seriously?

MARK: Pretty late, actually, like nineteen or twenty. I went to art school, studied graphic design and drawing. During that time, I was playing music with my band, too, just for fun. When I was young, I did all sorts of things; I directed some music videos—different creative stuff.

WAYNE: Then you put all that on hold and did the music thing, right? Your band was pretty successful.

MARK: Yeah, it was super fun. We toured all over the place for like ten years. But I always had this fantasy of being a painter, like maybe when I retired one day. I honestly didn't think that you could make a living as a painter.

WAYNE: Music is such a powerful thing, and when you play live in front of people, there's instant energy there. I'm picturing you sitting, painting alone, and there's no response until the thing is done and people can see it. What's that like?

MARK: That's true. The good thing now, for the most part, is social media. It really has changed the art scene. It provides instant feedback, which is awesome. It has really helped and encouraged me to keep going when I could see that people were enjoying my work.

WAYNE: As you started getting into painting, what was it like for you?

MARK: It was an interesting point. In 2005 or 2006, I was doing art on the side from my band stuff. I was loving jumping back into painting and doing more and more pieces. I did my first solo art show, and no one cared. Like, literally, no one came. It was really hard. But I kept at it.

WAYNE: How did a guy from France end up doing western art based on the early settling days of America?

MARK: When I was about thirty-five, I discovered this whole genre of art. And as I looked back at the work of some of the great masters, it just blew my mind. I was like, this is what I want to do. It just all started taking off from there. People sometimes ask me, "Do you get tired of painting horses and cowboys?" And I'm like, "No way!" I think there's an element, too, that being from France, the American spirit is so powerful, and the people that ventured out into these wild lands to make a life for themselves are so inspiring.

WAYNE: With my own artwork, it seems like I'm kind of bouncing around between four or five different styles. I like certain aspects of all of them but can't decide yet which one is really "me." Any thoughts on that for any art folks reading?

MARK: I think finding my style just came naturally at some point. When I was younger, I was all over the place. I loved Disney, anime, skateboarding art, classical paintings, mixed media—like, everything. Once I started doing western art, I honestly wasn't thinking about making a certain style consciously. It was just by years and years of working. I'd say, keep at it, and then one day you'll find it. And once you have it, go for it.

WAYNE: You've had some great successes here in the last couple years. People may look and say, "It must come easy to him. That guy probably never worries about anything, stresses over his art, or has a frustrating day." Any response to that?

MARK: [*laughs*] I wish. No, in everything, I think the most difficult thing is the uncertainty of the future. Just because people are excited about my work now doesn't mean they always will be. It's like life; it's always a faith step. There's nothing you can do about the future, or control, if the wind turns. You just have to keep doing what you're doing, and give it your very best. The older we get, I guess, the more we realize it's all very fragile.

WAYNE: I know you are married and a dad, too, correct? How do you juggle time being a dad and husband with your art dreams and goals?

MARK: On the time thing, it's actually a lot of crazy scheduling, and thank goodness we have some help. My wife is a photographer and she has shoots and stuff. Neither of our parents live anywhere near us, so sometimes it's a little crazy. But when we are all together, we want to really be together, to be present. (*There's an entire chapter on this coming up, as you'll see. It's interesting how this came up with so many people.*) Even with things like our phones, they can sure keep us from being present with someone. Just because we decide to not be on our phone doesn't mean the other person has decided to not be on theirs. Unless others do it, too, it can be a source of stress for sure. We want our kids to grow up knowing there's an amazing world out there that is outside of these devices.

WAYNE: So awesome, man. Thank you for your time. Okay, last question, and it's one I'm asking lots of the folks I'm chatting with. Ready? What would forty-two-year-old Mark Maggiori tell twenty-one-year-old Mark Maggiori?

MARK: I would try and appreciate things a little more. Be a little more grateful. I had to learn a lot the hard way when I was younger. I made a lot of decisions without honestly counting how they affected other people. I would also be more grateful and take the time to say things as simple as "Thank you."

# TARA ROYER STEELE

"I've learned to discern the difference between whether I'm tired or I'm
weary. If I'm tired, I can go take a nap, but if I'm weary, then that means
that this thing isn't producing joy or bearing fruit, and I pretty much need
to quit whatever it is. Yeah, weary means it's time to do something else."

Texas. Yes, we have a lot of pride. We are sort of our own country in our minds,
as you may know. We are big on freedom, and we definitely remember the
Alamo. Everything is bigger in Texas: the skies, the attitude, the love. There's
a T-shirt I designed and sell that features the outline of the state of Texas, and
inside it simply says, "YEP." It's usually the answer to the question.

If you are from the great state of Texas like me, the odds are pretty good that
you are aware of the town of Round Top. It's a quaint little place smack dab in
the middle of some of the most beautiful rolling hills in the state. Bluebonnets
flourish in the spring, and cows think they are pretty much in heaven.

The town with a population of just ninety swells with tens of thousands of
visitors twice a year during Round Top's Antiques Week. If you've never been,
come check it out. You'll discover miles and miles of tents full of treasures waiting
to be found as far as the eye can see. In Round Top it's not uncommon to see
Chip and Jo out there filming at Marburger Farm, or Matthew McConaughey
and designer wife Camila Alves shopping around. The Junk Gypsies from
HGTV have a super fun shop and lodging spot out there as well. The guys from
*Barnwood Builders*, the DIY Network show, have a shop there, too. If it's unique
personalities you're looking for, and tons of cool stuff, both new and old, this
is your spot.

For the past several years, I've had a booth out there with my art. Hands
down, what I love the most is the people. You just never know who you'll see
next. Folks from all over the country and even abroad visit this tiny town twice
a year for the festival. It's a huge Texas tradition. I've had colorful chats with
people from Ireland to Washington State. From sweet little ladies who live three
miles down the road to California designers. It's a blast.

Now, if you are at all familiar with any of the above, then you have heard of
the iconic Royers Café. Legendary is putting it mildly. The café maybe seats forty

or so. It's pretty common to see people gladly waiting outside for a table. It's not unusual to see former Texas Governor Rick Perry out there waiting for his table. The walls inside (and ceiling, for that matter) are literally covered with all sorts of goodies: Willie Nelson tour posters, Santa, old signs, quotes, signatures, Elvis stuff, and more than I could list here. You'll get lost, not only in the ambiance, but just wait until the food comes—amazing! This family institution is something that great movies are made of. Bud Royer, the patriarch, who years ago started this café, is awesome. Don't be surprised if you hear him yelling, "Orange handle!" to the newcomers who can't find their way out of the place! JB, his son, who now runs the café, is the king of their hand-battered buttermilk fried chicken. He is one of the kindest guys you'll ever meet. Tara, Bud's daughter, worked there for years until launching into her own spot, Pie Haven. Her pie will change your life. Seriously.

But what I love about Tara and Pie Haven is much more than the pie. It's been my joy to get to know Tara and her husband, Rick, over the past several years. I've been able to watch and be beyond encouraged by what she is doing with her business. If you visit Pie Haven, it'll only take you a nanosecond to realize that she is not there just to sell pie. This girl is peddling encouragement, y'all. Big time!

If you've visited, you know what the setup is there. Pie Haven operates out of a little old house, surrounded by huge old oak trees, in the middle of Henkel Square in the heart of Round Top. Under those trees are outdoor tables and chairs, most of which don't match, which adds to the character and just beckons you to come sit and relax (and have pie, obviously). As dusk falls, you'll see the lights that are strung up within those old trees come on. Pretty much amazing.

When you walk into that little shop, you'll see that the walls, like the ones at Royers Café, are covered. But they're covered with encouraging quotes, inspirational Bible verses, and quirky and hilarious sayings, most of which were done by hand by Tara. (By the way, she even has her own font out there!) You get the sense, after being in Pie Haven for just a few minutes, that Tara has her hand in every little detail in the place. From the hand-decorated, wooden ice-cream spoons to the "Not Today Satan" T-shirts, her creative handprint is all over her place, and the love comes through.

I was super excited when she agreed to have a sit-down chat with me for this book. When I think of the word *entrepreneur*, I think of Tara Royer. With Tara fresh off the heels of the release of her new book, *Eat, Pie, Love*, we connected for an interview at Pie Haven.

WAYNE: Tara! Woo hoo! This is awesome. Thank you for agreeing to chat for a bit. As you know, the Kerrs are big fans—not only of Royers, and Pie Haven, but of you, my friend. When I think of entrepreneurs, and of people fully being themselves, you came to my mind pretty quick. Let's get right to it. Here we go. On the days when you wake up and are like, "Okay, this is too much. I should just go to work for someone else. I could get a paycheck and not mess with all this 'stepping out into the unknown' all the time." This 'acceptance or rejection' world out there is too much today—much less the conversations that go on in our own minds. How do you turn the narrative around on those days?

TARA: Well, I tried working for someone else for three days . . .

WAYNE: [*laughing*] Yes!

TARA: So, seriously, I tried that. I worked at another restaurant (other than our family's) once for three days. I thought they were gonna have me do something fancy, and I was washing dishes. Now, don't get me wrong, I can wash dishes with the best of them. But I wondered pretty quickly, *Why would I go and wash someone else's dishes, when I could wash the dishes for my own business?* So, yeah, those days are gone. Now, just like anyone, there are days when I don't want to get up and go do the things I need to do and am called to do. But now I've learned to discern the difference between whether I'm tired or I'm weary. If I'm tired, I can go take a nap, but if I'm weary, then that means this thing isn't producing joy or bearing fruit. And I pretty much need to quit whatever it is. *Weary* means it's time to do something else.

WAYNE: Wow. Okay, interview over! So, give me a little of the back story of how you went from working with your family at Royers, to launching out into things on your own? Really, I guess my question is, when did the entrepreneurial seed in you come alive? What was the moment when you realized that you had creative ideas and visions that were your own, and you were ready to follow those?

TARA: Even when I was little bitty, I would make cookies and bread and take them into church. So, yeah, it's been in my bones I guess my whole life. I was working with my family for years at the café. But there was a time when, actually Rick (my husband) and I were in the trenches, and I realized that the café had become my identity. I had been somehow confined to those four walls in my heart. I had freedom there, for sure, to a certain degree, but I sensed a change was coming. Some developers were revamping the Henkel Square here in Round Top, and they approached Rick and me and said they'd love to have a coffee shop there. I was like, "Hey, okay, we know nothing about coffee, but we didn't really know anything about pie, either!" So, looking back, at the time it wasn't even something I knew I needed, but we felt like God was opening the way for us to fully step into something we could make our own. I had the chance to make the place my own. I could walk in and fully be myself.

WAYNE: I've told so many people that when you walk into Pie Haven, you can feel the love. You can see your imagination and handprint over every little thing. I've heard you say before that you just wanted to create a place for people to have real and meaningful conversations; a place for people to connect.

TARA: As I look back, I wasn't really deep in walking with God. But this was the beginning of me shedding all the layers that I felt like the world had added to my heart. To this day, when I walk in our building, I still get giddy and excited. To be able to walk into the place where you work, and it brings you joy—it's a huge blessing. I know that not everyone gets to say that. I'm very thankful.

WAYNE: And nowadays, there's much more happening with you than the Pie Haven.

TARA: Yeah, it's crazy to see how it has all evolved. People used to say to me, "You should write a book!" I never thought it would actually happen. The podcast as well. We all have these areas in our hearts where we might secretly say, "I'd love to do that one day." And to be able to walk in that, and put my own spin on it, is awesome.

WAYNE: What's a funny or crazy story about something that has happened since you've been at all this?

TARA: Let's see . . . when Rick and I were just dating, we were catering a huge wedding. My mom was with us in Rick's truck—his very brand-new truck—and my dad was driving our big catering truck. We were at the venue getting ready, and, well, somehow I locked Rick's truck with the keys still inside. Everything we needed to finish the deal was in there. Rick was trying feverishly to get it open. Back in those days with Chevy, if you tried to Slim Jim the lock open, it would lock back instantly. Rick was trying, and meanwhile my dad was screaming, "Just break the glass!" And I was screaming, "I just met this guy, and it's his new truck!"

Everyone was inside the church, and they were literally about to open the doors and come out. Rick was remaining calm and trying to get the thing open. Meanwhile, I was thinking we were about to ruin these peoples' wedding. It was a beautiful day, everything had been perfect, except for this. I started praying, "God, please help us out on this!" My dad was about to break the glass, and Rick said he would try *one* last time. Literally, miraculously, he popped the unlock button, and in that exact second, the church doors flew open. The walk-out music was blaring! We grabbed everything, and nobody had a clue any of that stuff ever happened.

WAYNE: Okay, one last question. This is something I've been asking most folks I connect with during this year. What would you tell twenty-year-old Tara?

TARA: Oh, no! *[laughing]*

WAYNE: Okay, let me rephrase. In terms of going for it, pursuing your own dreams, that train of thought. What would you say to your younger self? Or, what would you say to the fifteen-year-old girl reading this book?

TARA: Hmmm . . . I would tell a fifteen-year-old girl reading this book, that whatever the "thing" is that keeps coming up in your gut or in your heart, that is not coming from other people. I believe that those are straight God-given desires. Don't let the layers of this world and the people of the world smash those. Don't let other people dictate your hopes and dreams. Just stand in what God's truth is, not what everyone else's truth is. I know that fifteen-year-old me sure needed to hear that.

WAYNE: Thank you so much, Tara. Proud of you, my friend.

As I was driving home from my meeting with Tara, I thought about how I have a front row seat into the uniqueness of our two little girls. Each is blonde with blue-green eyes. But that is where the similarities stop. I was reminded of this last year on Valentine's Day. I had gone into a local shop to get something for my sweet little Valentines. I walked up to the counter with the two stuffed animals I had picked out. I said, "These are for my two little girls; I actually have three Valentines at home." The lady behind the checkout counter said, "Awe, that's sweet. And you clearly have two very different little girls!"

The moment she said that I looked at the two stuffed animals with new eyes. Until she shared her observation, I hadn't noticed how different those stuffed animals were. I had picked a white and gray kitten for Elliott, who is very serene and loves to read. Her kitten had seemed calm, tender, and sweet. Elliott would go on to name her "Gray Snowflake."

Emory's gift was a hippo wearing a purple tie-dyed shirt, striped pants, a tutu, and orange shoes. Emory would cleverly call her, "Tutu Colorful." Perfect. You see, our sweet Emory is a whirlwind bundle of joy, energy, laughter, and smiles, and this matches her to a T. This girl brings sunshine into every day. These days find me watching Emory roll through the house on her brightly colored roller skates. Her life is in fact "too, too colorful." And you know what? I want both of my girls, who have the keys to my heart, to live to the fullest.

The Bible says the same thing about my unique girls that it does about you: You are fearfully and wonderfully made (Psalm 139:14).

I'll unpack this more the further we go on this journey together. I hope that reading from my conversations with people who are braving—living out their individual callings—will inspire you to embrace yours.

You have a dream.

I know you do.

I think someone placed that dream in your heart, and what's super cool is that, most likely, it's for purposes bigger than you.

## SOME THINGS TO KICK AROUND

At the end of each of the chapters in *Braving* you will find a few questions. They're meant to give you a few minutes to ponder what you've read, to do some self-reflection, and to dig around in the soil of your heart to see what you unearth. Grab a pen and make some notes. There are no right or wrong answers here; just take advantage of some space for you to journal your thoughts in response to the questions.

1. When I talked about "being fully you," what came up in your heart?

_____

_____

_____

_____

_____

2. If you are being honest, how do you think people describe you?

_____

_____

_____

_____

_____

3. If you are being honest, how do you describe yourself?

_____

_____

_____

_____

_____

_____

_____

4. Is there anything, anyone, or any behavior that is holding you back from being the real you?

_____

_____

_____

_____

_____

_____

_____

## chapter two

# SEE YOUR LIFE AS A STORY

"Then something Tookish woke up inside him, and he wished to go and see the great mountains, and hear the pine-trees and the waterfalls, and explore the caves, and wear a sword instead of a walking-stick."[7]

—J.R.R. Tolkien, *The Hobbit*

Whether you realize it or not, you are smack-dab in the middle of an epic story. Epic! You were born into a certain time in history at a certain place in the world, and with certain giftings that no one else on the planet has. As it turns out, you are living in one of the most amazing times in human history. Also, this could be one of history's most challenging times for the human soul and heart.

Each and every day, you and I make choices that will steer how our story may go. To me, this reminds me of a rudder on a large ship. Turn it only one degree, and over time the direction of that ship is heading to a completely different location. Yes, there are tons of things about my journey on this ship that can't be controlled.

*Will my ship be heading into a huge hurricane in two days? Does my crew have what it takes to get there as a team? What if we get scurvy? (Is that still a thing on the open sea?) Will there be pirates waiting for our ship?*

All out of my control.

As I am writing this today (in April 2020) the world is in the midst of the coronavirus pandemic. Talk about something that is out of our control. Tens of thousands have died, millions are out of work. Grocery stores are sold out of everything from milk to toilet paper. All sporting events are canceled, school is canceled, Broadway is closed, Disneyland is even closed, for Pete's sake. The stock market (as of today) is down 35 percent from a month ago. And yesterday, the price of oil went to below zero.[8] Not sure how that is even possible. The virus is serious, and my prayers are with anyone who is impacted. Everyone— well, not everyone, but a *big* chunk of people—is panicking. People have been told to stay in their homes, and not even go out to see loved ones. On top of all that, there are racial tensions and riots in America, even as we draw near the presidential election. This is a historic time that we are all slap in the middle of.

If I'm honest, it seems odd to be compiling all of these interviews to inspire you, the reader, to be brave in pursuing what makes you come alive, in these times. But perhaps it's a better time than ever to be talking about braving. Right now, we have to be brave to just go to the grocery store. We have to be brave to think about how we will survive the financial hardship. We have to be brave to turn on the news and see what else could be happening.

At my local church, where I lead worship, we started doing what many churches are doing—livestreaming our service. Last week, I stood on the stage with my team leading worship in front of 1,500 empty seats. At that moment, I knew these three things deep in my heart:

1. I am in the middle of a huge story right now.

2. There are possibly thousands of people watching online, and I want them to be encouraged, and for us all to turn our hearts to God.

3. It's okay that there are no people here, because this worship is directed toward God, not people. God is bigger than this virus. He is faithful, and I can trust Him completely.

The truth, my friend, is that you and I are in the middle of an amazing story. Can you see it? One that is full of highs and lows. Once a few months or years go by, what will have happened in this saga? Will the coronavirus of 2020 have gotten worse? Will it be forgotten already? Who knows? What I do know is this: Our story will continue. Your story will continue. Seeing your life as a story will help you own it more fully and navigate it more purposefully.

There will be mountains and valleys. Will you press past your fears into the wide-open range of your dreams? Will you let fear, or the voices of others, dictate whether you press on or turn back?

If you will begin to see your life as a story—your story—I believe many things will start becoming clearer in your heart. You have one life to live on this earth and for only a certain amount of time. Sure enough, parts of the story are out of your control. Much of it, though, is right there in your own hands.

When a person sets out to drive from Katy, Texas to Albuquerque, New Mexico, for an art festival, he has a lot of time to think. Thirteen hours and forty-seven minutes to be exact. I was heading westward to the Rio Grande Arts and Crafts Festival. My truck was packed to the brim with paintings, prints, greeting cards, a backdrop, and a desk—everything but the kitchen sink. Life is an ever-evolving adventure, right? For those who are braving, the answer is "yes."

I had been on the road about eight hours when I received a text message. The art festival had officially been canceled due to worries over the coronavirus. This was at the point when many events were starting to shut down. So, I pulled over to a gas station to consider my next steps. *Do I stop for the night here and rest, and then drive home tomorrow? Or, if I just turn around and head back, I'll be home when my girls wake up in the morning.* The second option seemed much better, even though it turned into a sixteen-hour driving day. I don't recommend it.

But while I was driving back, something pretty cool happened. An entire story unfolded in my mind, as if I were watching a movie. It was the story of two mustangs and how they were each wired differently. I'm not sure if it had been partially inspired by my talks with Ben Masters a few months beforehand, or inspired by too many green teas while driving. I think God dropped this story into my heart for a reason. I would love to share it with you here.

# THE TALE OF TWO MUSTANGS
## part one

Once there were two mustangs. They had a good and easy life. They slept in a nice barn at night and had all the hay and water they could ever want. Life at the wood mill was good.

Every day was pretty much the same. Each morning their owner would greet them in the early hours. They would be placed in front of a large wooden cart, tied in, and yoked to one another.

It was their job each day to carry the cut wood from the mill all the way into town. With a crack of the whip and at the sound of "Haw!", they were off. In no time, the two mustangs would reach a nice trot. They could easily pull the heavy load. In the morning fog, the team and cart followed the dirt road that meandered through the rolling hills.

Each day, the route was the same. Over the eastern rolling hills, through the overarching line of oak trees that led into the open glade, past the long stone wall, and finally, across the creek bridge into town. These mustangs could probably make this delivery with their eyes closed.

On this particularly cold and foggy morning, the team hitched up and was on their way. They went past the rolling hills. They knew the high, majestic, cathedral-like entryway into the oak tree forest was coming next.

The morning sun was up now and shooting hundreds of shafts of light through the canopy. Steam was rising from the breath of both the mustangs and the driver. It was a marvelous sight.

As they made the turn, exiting the oak tree forest and heading into the open glade, a sound in the distance cut through the morning air. It briefly caught the mustangs off guard, for they recognized the sound right away. A herd of wild mustangs was on the move.

They could not be seen, but judging by the sound of it, there must have been fifteen to twenty of them. The sound of their hooves on the ground, along with their whinnying and neighing, was creating quite a symphony.

As the team and cart came fully into the glade, they could see the herd on the horizon. It sounded quite like thunder in the distance. One of the two mustangs had never seen a sight like this and was in awe. The other mustang, the older of the two, had seen them several times and simply acknowledged them with an uninterested nod while continuing to pull his half of the cart. The team didn't miss a step and kept right on pulling as the driver gave a few more cracks of the whip to keep them focused on the job at hand. They reached the five-foot-tall stone wall that ran along the roadside, and then the team got a good look at the wild herd.

The wild mustangs had stopped for a moment, as if taking note of this strange cart in motion. In an instant, the herd rose up, kicking up dust, and then off they tore. They went splashing through the creek and bounded up across the other side. Just like that, they were completely out of sight.

A short while later, the two mustangs and cart arrived in town, and the delivery of boards was made. These boards were going to help build the very first school house in town, a new church building, and even a boardwalk in front of the post office. Both mustangs felt a sense of pride in the work they were a part of.

The run back to the mill that afternoon was slower, and much easier on the team with the weight of the delivery now all gone.

Once into their stalls for the evening, the first mustang simply could not get the picture that he had seen that day out of his mind. *Mustangs could run free? What does it feel like to run with so many of them, through the water, and up into the high country? What is it like to never have a whip at your back? What is it like to sleep under stars instead of inside a corral?*

That night this mustang did not sleep. The other mustang was asleep before you could say, "Frog went a-courtin' and he did ride."

The next morning their owner came to get them ready again for the day's delivery. As usual, he placed them in front of the large wooden cart, tied them in, and yoked them to one another. With a hearty "Haw!" and a crack of the whip, they were off again. The sky that day was a crystal clear blue, and the air was crisp. The first mustang wondered and even hoped that he might see the herd once more. The route was the same. Over the eastern rolling hills, through the overarching line of oak trees, around the bend, and into the open glade.

As the team came around the turn, the same sound echoed through the valley as it had yesterday. Indeed, the herd was on the move again. The first mustang felt a rush of excitement and actually started pulling too quickly. "Steady now!" screamed the driver.

This time the herd was at a full sprint as they came into the open valley. There were almost too many to count. Large, strong, and wild. Some were brown, some were spotted, some were black, and all were beautiful. Unkempt manes flowing in the wind and the dust flying, not a single saddle, strap, or harness could be seen on any of them.

The first mustang was so overcome with the scene, all he really thought was, *I have to be with them. I was made to be with them!* As the duo traveled the road, which began to border the five-foot-high stone wall, the herd ran alongside at the same speed as the cart. The only thing separating the dust storm of this wild herd and the team was the stone wall.

"Whoa!" cried the driver, as the team instinctively matched the pace of the wild herd. But it was no use, they were now in an all-out sprint.

The first mustang reared up and bucked. With this one motion, he broke away from one of the straps tying him into the team.

"Hold!" screamed the driver.

The team slowed to a halt, as the first mustang bucked again, then totally broke free from the cart. He ran alongside the stone wall, the wild herd running on the other side. The herd circled back around for another pass along the wall, and the one mustang followed suit. Suddenly, he heard the whooshing of a rope by his head, as the driver was tossing his lasso to try and catch the freed mustang. Barely missing, he tried a second time to land his toss.

The herd was now stomping and screaming as they ran, and the dust they were kicking up was like a sandstorm. The sound they made was like thunder and drove birds away in every direction. With one last pass along the long stone wall, the wild herd whinnied and snorted as they flew by.

The first mustang, the one free from the cart, was at full stride alongside the wild herd, with only the wall separating them. He looked and saw the end of the stone wall coming quickly.

And he jumped . . .

That is not the end of the story. Later, we will pick up where this left off.

But let me pause here and ask, how does this story make you feel? Does it stir something to life in you?

Are you thinking that the mustang who broke away is crazy, or that he is about to be on the adventure of a lifetime?

Let me be clear here, this allegory is what I saw in my imagination one day. I don't believe the story means, "The grass is always greener," or "I'm tired of my job, so I'll quit and pursue a fantasy." Or, worse yet, "This relationship I am in seems boring, so I'm leaving." No, in fact, a powerful and true statement I have heard is, "The grass grows where you water it."

What I pray is that this story stirs in you an idea. For some of us, deep in our souls, in our spirit, we know there is more out there for us than what we are settling for. Maybe you have a dream long held that you have suppressed, maybe because of your own doubts, or maybe because of something someone said to you or over you. If you are a person who feels they have so dumbed down and numbed down their dream or vision, then I am talking to you. I am here to deliver this message to you: You can do it!

Today is a Wednesday. Two separate times today I heard something insanely similar from two different people. Firstly, I was getting coffee this morning at a local coffeeshop, and I asked the woman behind the counter how it was going for her today. She replied, "At least it's Wednesday. My week is half over." Then, a few moments later, I said "Hello" to someone and asked how they were doing. His response was, "My week is halfway over, so I'm good."

Is this the life that many of us have resigned to? To do work that many of us don't really even care about, trudging through our days so that we can get to the weekend? No. Quite possibly, a long time ago, you took your dream, put it in a box, locked it, placed it in a closet, and shut the door.

My friend, I believe you can do and be more than you ever dreamed. As I mentioned earlier, one of my favorite Bible verses over the years has been Ephesians 2:10. Every time anyone ever asked me to sign a CD or T-shirt or anything, I would write this verse and encourage them to look it up. May I share it with you again? "For we are God's masterpiece. He has created us anew in Christ Jesus, so we can do the good things he planned for us long ago" (NLT).

You may think, *Wait, what? I'm a masterpiece? No, that's not what my number of Instagram followers says. That's not what my family might say, or friends, or whomever.* But, yes, you are. And you are right in the middle of a story. Your story. And we are all part of a much bigger story.

## SOME THINGS TO KICK AROUND

1. How does the story of the two mustangs make you feel?

_____

_____

_____

_____

_____

_____

2. Are you thinking that the mustang who breaks free is crazy, or that he is about to be on the adventure of a lifetime?

_____

_____

_____

_____

_____

_____

3. If you're being honest, what are some things about your own story that have been hard? Does something stir and come alive in you when you think of a dream you hold dearly?

_____

_____

_____

_____

_____

_____

4. What are some things that you are still believing and hoping for? Take a risk here, and write out your dreams. The first step is being brave enough to name them! You can do it!

_____

_____

_____

_____

_____

_____

## chapter three
# DEFEAT DOUBT AND JUMP

"The ceiling of my potential is the floor of the God room."[9]

—John Maxwell

When our daughter Elliott was about three and a half, she had just gotten a handle on the whole swimming thing. She had been swimming without floaties all summer long and was doing a great job.

Our family went to a community pool in our neighborhood, and E wanted to play around in the kids' pool. My wife had sweet Emory, who was one and a half at the time, in her arms. After a few minutes, Elliott wanted to get in the big pool and give it a try. She stood ankle-deep on the pool steps, stepped down a few feet into the water, swam around, and then swam back to the steps. This was all totally within her comfort zone.

But then she asked if she could swim from the steps to the side edge of the pool. I said, "Sure," but I kept an eagle eye on her. Well, instead of swimming toward the side, which was about eight feet away, she launched out heading toward the very middle of the pool and the deep end. I said, "Hey, Elliott, come back in this direction." She couldn't really hear me, as she was partially under water, not to mention all the people and noise out there was distracting. She kept going. "Elliott!" I shouted.

Next thing I knew, I had tossed my cell phone out of my pocket and jumped in the pool—fully dressed. I swam out and valiantly saved my offspring. It was like a scene from a movie. I could almost hear the heroic theme music playing as I brought her back to the steps.

Well, that's at least how I saw it. Many of the people at the pool looked at me with astonishment. Most of the moms present had a slight smile and a healthy dose of pity for me. My wife was just shaking her head, laughing.

Elliott had actually been doing fine with her swimming. She hadn't needed her helicopter dad to swoop in at that point. (But I would do it again in a heartbeat.) Elliott had not made a mistake swimming in that direction; she had done it on purpose. She had defeated her doubt and was going for it. She knew her mommy and daddy were close by. She knew she had been taught how to dog paddle, float, hold her breath, and move her arms so that she kept moving forward. The only person freaking out in this situation was me. She had defeated her doubt and had jumped.

In this chapter, I'll share from my interviews with people who are doing just that—defeating doubt and jumping. From leaving a suburban home to become homesteaders who are committed to living debt-free, to leaving an office job to work full time as a musician. From selling your house and taking your family RV-ing across the country for a full year, to chucking the status quo to becoming a guide in Alaska. These are some through-the-roof inspiring folks you are about to meet.

I'm talking about jumping into meaningful work, not chasing after money or fame.

I'm talking about looking your fears right in the face and punching them in the nose.

I'm talking about getting up off the couch and making a difference in someone else's life and your own.

I'm talking about acknowledging that there's a dream in your heart, and it has the powerful potential to be more than just a dream.

Steps have to be taken to turn your dream into a reality. If you think someone is going to randomly knock on your door and hand you the keys to make it happen, you're completely in La La Land. Check out what these folks have to say, and you'll be inspired to defeat the doubt and jump, too.

## BEAU BROTHERTON

> "Don't tell yourself you'll never do or accomplish something.
> Rather, ask, 'How can I?'"

Beau and Kelly Brotherton and their four kids live in a shed.

Well, not really a shed, but a shed that has been converted into a house. I've known these guys for several years and count them as some of my dearest friends. When this book started swimming around in my head, I felt they sure needed to be a part of it, and I knew that they perfectly belonged in this chapter about defeating doubt and jumping.

The Brothertons have a YouTube channel called "Better Together Life," with over 100,000 followers and nearly 12 million views. This is Texas homesteading at its finest. They host a Facebook group called "Shed to House," with tons of followers as well. This family is pursuing their dream of being completely debt-free in their thirties and they are right on track to make it happen. Beau, Kelly, and their four kiddos live in a 768-square-foot home here in central Texas that is full of love, joy, honest ups and downs, and tons of laughter. They are self-employed and homeschool their kids on top of that! They are certainly braving. They inspire me as they challenge the status quo. It took courage for them to defeat doubt and jump into what some might consider a radical lifestyle. I caught up with my friend Beau for a brief chat over the phone.

**WAYNE:** I know much of y'all's story, but tell me how in the world you guys went from living in a home in the suburbia of Katy, Texas, to living in a shed on eight acres. I guess, more important than *how* is *why* you did it. Tell me your story!

**BEAU:** What a journey it's been. I guess, to back up, it began when Kelly and I started realizing that we had a dream in our hearts. We wanted to be self-employed, debt-free, and able to homeschool our kiddos. How in the world does anyone do that? We also started realizing that if we stayed in our current home setup, we would not become debt-free for a long time. That also meant that we had to keep working more to pay for the house. Then by working more, the odds of us being able to homeschool were not looking good. It is all a spiral, and we just were not happy with living our lives like that. We knew something was brewing in our hearts.

Then I started meeting these weird and strange people who were living off the grid. They were talking about our food systems, our economic system, and how super fragile it all actually is. A weatherman doesn't love a hurricane coming, but says to everyone, "Hey, heads up, this is happening." But the bigger thing really was that we knew our current setup living in suburbia wasn't good for us, and so we went for it!

WAYNE: I know you've said that one of your priorities, too, was to be able to let your boys run wild and free, out in nature, and not be raised in the modern suburbs. I'd guess lots of people might share this dream. How did you guys go from "idea" to actually making it happen?

BEAU: It's the greatest thing ever seeing my kids running all over the place, covered in mud half the time, chasing animals as well as each other. I got lucky in the fact that I saw a niche in this "Shed to House" movement that's happening. When we launched our little Facebook group, it took off. We went from zero to 60,000 followers in just six months. I think part of the charm of this whole thing is that we are transparent with our ups and downs on this journey, and we share our failures on our YouTube channel.

WAYNE: I laughed so hard when I watched the newest video you posted this past week. You were out behind your home and were all set to drill what looked like post holes. You had these huge earphones on, protective eyewear, and the camera was rolling. Off you went, and your wife was in the frame as well, working on something. Next thing you know, you turned off the big drill, looked down into the hole, looked again, and then threw off your headphones and walked off while the audio was being bleeped out.

Kelly calmly walked over to the hole, looked in, and said, "Yep, that line you just cut used to give us Internet. Oh well, we can spend less time on social media."

I think people appreciate that you guys don't pretend to have it all figured out, and that you're learning as you go—together.

BEAU: It's been an incredible journey. Not always easy, but amazing. I had no clue of so many things along the way, but we were in it to learn. Still are. From clearing the land, to putting the road in, to building out the shed, it's been an experience. In financial terms, we work really hard with multiple streams of income so that we can have quality time to be with our family, and also be self-sustaining. We monetize from our sponsors online, we have an e-book, the YouTube channel. We are not fully self-sustained or anything food-wise, but we have an amazing garden, chickens, pigs, and rabbits. This gives us all kinds of safety nets, with food, income, everything. I haven't bought eggs from a store in over a year. I tell you what, I have a huge respect now for where all of the food we consume comes from. I've learned how hard farming really is. People think it would be great to have land and animals. Guess what? Animals destroy grass like crazy.

We just did this whole thing one step at a time. We prayed about where to buy land. Once we found our spot, it was baby steps. I had friends, relatives, anyone I could find come out and help us clear land. Then we put a small road in, ran power out there. The fun thing is that we filmed this whole journey, mistakes and all. So we were, and still are, sharing the joy and the challenges along the way. As people started following our journey online, we saw that this had potential to be bigger than we even dreamed. We're showing all the good and bad about moving your family of six into a converted shed.

**WAYNE:** In this section of *Braving*, we are talking about "defeating the doubt and jumping." You guys sure have done that. What have been some of the highs and lows in all this so far?

**BEAU:** I think all the time with our family these past two years has been worth more than all the money in the world. God has rebuilt so many aspects of our lives through this adventure. Everett, my boy, used to literally be afraid of animals. He has such confidence now, it's amazing.

I think some of the more challenging things have been how our marriage has been stretched. We built and designed a shed together for Pete's sake. Let me just say, building a house with your wife, you don't really know what marriage is until you try something like that. For sure, this doesn't work for everyone. Some people may think if you move, you'll run away from the problems, but we all know that's not true. My wife is a superhero and this has been the greatest for our family.

In terms of defeating the doubt and jumping, I honestly think that we have just gotten to the point where we do that over and over and over again. We often coach people, and we have seen this often. They will try something new, and when they fail, they bail out. They quit. Those who keep following through without giving up will succeed.

**WAYNE:** Huge. What is some practical advice you might suggest to the person reading this to help them have this mentality? They may be eyeing a dream or venture of their own. How can they direct that dream so it heads toward becoming reality?

**BEAU:** I think Dave Ramsey said something like this, "Everybody has a pie in the sky dream, but it's in the sky. You can't actually put it into action; it's too overwhelming. You have to bring it down out of the sky, into a vision you can actually see." For me, a huge principle is to not say, "This thing will never happen," but instead to say, "How can I make this happen?" I literally write that idea down on paper. I may not have the answer right away—I might be doing the dishes or lying in bed—and boom! The ideas start to come. For real, it's like we have a crazy computer or something in between our ears. I think God designed it so that we can have our minds actually brainstorming a solution to something in the background, even if we are not focusing on trying to solve it.

My wife, Kelly, has this saying. "There are dreamers that dream, and there are dreamers that do." That's truly so much of it. Don't tell yourself you'll never do or accomplish something. Rather, ask "How can I?" Break the dream down into a vision. Then break the vision down into goals. Then break those goals down into action tasks.

I was taken aback when I was doing another interview a few weeks ago. The guy said, "Wow, Beau, you are thirty-eight years old and you will be completely debt-free by the end of the year. You will be debt-free in your thirties!" When he said that, I was blown away. And I was reminded that it actually had been one of my goals. Unreal. It takes real work, but it's so worth it.

**WAYNE:** Okay, Beau, last question for you today. What would thirty-eight-year-old Beau tell twenty-year-old Beau?

His answer honestly blew me away.

**BEAU:** You know what? I don't think I'd tell him anything. Nope. I wouldn't change a thing. The process of learning and growing, and failing and overcoming, has been the ride of a lifetime. I'm worried that if I tell twenty-year-old Beau something, he'd screw it up! No, I'm a huge believer that God's overall plan is good. I'm not happy because this homestead thing is happening, I'm happy to just realize where God has me now. I really can live a life that is fully joyful and content.

The Brothertons inspire me. They make me smile. They defeated their doubts and jumped— And guess what, they are still jumping each day. They encourage me, and I hope they encourage you, too.

You really can take your dream from being a "pie in the sky" wish and, with hard work, determination, and prayer, make it a reality. The Brothertons remind me that our dream is not the answer to us finding peace and happiness. Our dream can actually become an unhealthy thing if it becomes what our entire universe revolves around.

One of the statements that Beau made that hit me in the most practical way was his example of writing goals out for himself. I remember my last "day job" from years ago before jumping into the music world. It was with a supermarket chain in Texas named Fiesta. I was a graphic designer for them and made ads for the weekly newspaper. (Not the most creative thing I've ever done, but I learned a ton.) One of the most memorable things from that time is that they sent us to a huge one-day conference. At that event, I heard, coming from one of the speakers, someone sharing a crazy statistic with us. He said that in the United States, less than 3 percent of people write down their own goals. Yes, you read it correctly.

Another mind-blowing way to say it is that 97 percent of people *do not* write down goals for themselves.[10] And on top of that, even less than 3 percent put them up on their wall, where they will see them every day.

Beau had theorized why. He suggested that many people have never really heard of the practice of writing down their goals, which I believe. But for most people, the reason they don't do it is that it's scary. Who wants to write down a list of things that they aren't accomplishing yet? Much less put it up on a wall? This seems like no fun at all, but here's the thing, just like Beau mentioned, and I've seen it in my own life, when you write your goals down, it forces your brain to break the steps toward achieving them down into manageable bites.

The year I was working with Fiesta, I was doing music at some camps and a concert here and there. Each event was so powerful and inspiring, there was no going back for me. I knew in my gut that music was the direction I was heading. At least, that was what my heart was telling me as I kept going back, every single Monday morning, to my little cubical.

I remember one week in particular when I was asked to lead the music for a full week of camp during summer. "Of course!" I said. I took my remaining vacation time to go to this camp. All week it was incredible. Being with students, playing sand volleyball, and eating in a cafeteria. Are you kidding me? Awesome!

Campfires, laughter, powerful teaching, and inspiring stories from the Bible were being shared. I remember thinking that the speaker probably thinks that the messages were for all the kids, but he was speaking directly to my heart, too. When the week came to a close, kids were saying goodbye to each other, and to me. Real, meaningful, and even life-changing things had happened in only five short days. People were exchanging contact information and shedding tears.

I remember the feeling as clear as day on the following Monday morning. I drove up to the Fiesta corporate office, and I put my tie on in my truck. I walked to my cubical and sat down. Pretty much immediately, I thought, *No way*. I'd realized that, for me, being with and investing in people was way more of my heartbeat.

That very week, I started investigating this "write you goals down" thing.

I went and bought a huge piece of white poster board and taped it up on my bedroom wall, positioned perfectly so I would see it first thing after waking up. I wrote down goals that were huge, and below them put the action steps that would have to happen before the goal could become a reality.

For example, I wrote down: "Full-time musician in one year." Great. Sounded awesome. But below that were the action steps that had to happen first. Things like, "Save enough to buy a small, portable sound system," "Play two to three events per month," "Start investigating and saving for the recording of my first album," and so on. Being somewhat of an artistic kind of person, I would draw a little illustration next to each item, just so I could see it in my mind. Something that I literally still do today is put a box in front of each item. I know it's old school, but I draw one line from corner to corner through the box if the item has gotten started. If it has been accomplished, then I add a second line to the box, making an *X* and marking the item as complete.

Let me tell you, there's nothing like looking at a vision board like this when you can cross something off that you've accomplished. Then immediately I add the next goal item. I remember that on the list where I'd written ". . . two to three events per month," once this step was being fulfilled steadily, I changed the aim to read, ". . . five events every month." Six months later, I had scratched that off and had written, ". . . eight events per month, and six full weeks of camps this summer." I was then taking that dream from somewhere up in the sky and bringing it down to earth.

There's some crazy cool truth to what Beau mentioned. Once you put down a goal, it unlocks some part of your heart, or brain, or imagination, and lets them work on your behalf.

I have seen my goal wall reflect what sounds like some crazy things over the years—"Perform live 180 days per year," "Sing in Japan," "Pay off truck," "Radio airplay," "Save for wedding ring!"—all of which I saw happen. Not by luck, or just talent, or anything, but by following through and working hard.

Lastly, there's something huge that's a part of this, I believe. At the top of my other goals, I always put things that can never be truly "marked off." For me, there are character aims that are always a work in progress. These are things I might write as, "Walk closely with God," "Be a giver," and "Read God's Word." I might "accomplish" these things on a given day. But, guess what? The next day I wake up again. What good would it be for me to make some of these goals happen, but then become self-centered? What good would it be for me to cross off a bunch of to-do items and not love my neighbor very well? So, these are aims that are literally placed at the top of my goal wall, never to be crossed out, because they're part of a lifelong journey.

Are you inspired yet? Are you ready to write some goals down on paper that have been left dormant in your heart for months, or years, or decades? Try it. Your dream may not be homesteading or to become a full-time musician, but your dream is big. Go for it.

P.S. They say that things are "caught, not taught" when it comes to your kids. My little girl Elliott just came by and showed me something she is working on. It was *her* goal list! The list includes, but is not limited to, reading two hundred books, running a 10K, having ten cats, writing her own book, and much more. Go, girl.

# AINSLIE GROSSER

> "I'm of two minds on this. As someone who is not from this country, I can speak to this, I think. One of the downsides to the 'American Dream' thing is that if you're not 'living your dream,' then you're not living. I was just listening to Ecclesiastes this morning, and Solomon was basically saying unless you find joy in the journey you're having, you're not gonna find it when you reach your destination."

This guy right here, y'all.

I connected with Ainslie about ten years ago when I was looking for the right person to mix my latest album. He is an award-winning engineer who has worked on truckloads of hit records, many Grammy-winning. But most importantly, being from Australia, he has a super cool Aussie accent. Ainslie has mixed the last of my four albums (still waiting on *my* Grammy). On top of all that, his heart is amazing.

Actually, the reason I reached out to him had nothing to do with music. I wanted to talk to him about the new adventure that he is currently on with his family. You want to talk about taking a faith step and jumping? About four months ago he and his family sold their Nashville home, sold his studio mixing console, and tons of audio gear, and bought a huge RV and trailer. Now they travel across the country, homeschooling their kiddos, while he literally continues to mix hit records on his laptop with in-ear monitors! What a ride this family is on.

I spoke with Ainslie on the phone—and yes, he was driving his RV.

**WAYNE:** Ainslie! Dude, tell me about this journey that you guys are on. Wow!

**AINSLIE:** Yep, mate, there's a fine line between brave and crazy.

**WAYNE:** Okay, so I need to hear the story of how you guys decided to do this adventure as a family.

**AINSLIE:** One day we looked up and all of a sudden we felt trapped. I'm the luckiest guy in the world to be able to do what I do—mix records and work in the music industry. It's what I love. But once we got to the point of having a big house with all the trappings, it was like, I *have* to get the money. I *have* to make music just to keep things going. I could tell it was starting to sap the joy from my heart, and I was just making music for the money. It's not a cool feeling. At the same time, our kiddos were struggling a little bit in school. With the work and stress of all of it, we felt conflicted. I started thinking about our greatest times as a family when I was growing up. The great highlights of my childhood were traveling together as a family. Our family always thrives when we are outside, exploring, seeing, and learning new things.

At the same time, technology has literally changed so much that I can do what I do mixing-wise on a laptop with good in-ear monitors. Honestly, even five years ago, this wasn't possible. The idea came to our heads, and I looked at my wife and said, "Can we?" Next thing you knew, we were checking out all these people online who were living on the road in an RV—and even doing it with their kids. A year later, here we are. We sold our house, my mixing console, most of our stuff. New chapter together!

**WAYNE:** This is amazing. Are you guys on the road right now?

**AINSLIE:** *[laughing]* I'm literally driving now. We are somewhere in Tennessee between two state parks.

**WAYNE:** What has been the greatest, "Yes, this is awesome!" moment, and the most "Oh my gosh. What have we done?" moment?

**AINSLIE:** The greatest moments so far have been seeing my kids flourish outside. When things all come together and there are other kids around, and its sunny, sitting at some Florida beach, riding our bikes, it's amazing. We are all on our phones less; it's honestly unbelievable some days. I'm able to work outdoors in a park or under the stars. Our family sitting and talking as the sun is setting over the ocean, amazing memories are being made already.

The other side of that question: What have been some of the downsides? Let me list just a few for you: Our generator has blown up. Oil leaks. We've had to be towed three times. We've been stuck four times. Three collisions (not all my fault, by the way). And thousands of dollars in repairs, so far. What else would you like to know? It's not all beer and skittles, as we say in Australia.

**WAYNE:** Wowza. That's real right there.

When I asked Ainslie the next question, it was so very profound to me, it struck me to the core. His answer literally reminded me how important it has been for me to write this book and for you to read this book. Please, do me a favor: Take a deep breath right now, and pause. Read the following in an undistracted way and receive this insight. It's huge.

**WAYNE:** What advice would you give to anyone considering "jumping" into a dream they have? Any guidance for someone who is right on the edge of going for it; what would you say to them?

**AINSLIE:** I'm of two minds on this. As someone who is not from this country, I can speak to this, I think. One of the downsides to the American Dream is that if you're not "living your dream," then you're not living. I was just listening this morning to Ecclesiastes, and Solomon was basically saying, unless you find joy in the journey you're having, you're not gonna find it when you reach your destination. The more you seek, the less you will find. And I think that can be true with dreams, too. If you have a dream that you can achieve, go for it; I'm not saying don't do it. But if you're unhappy without that dream, you're probably gonna be unhappy with that dream.

Happiness isn't about fulfilling your dreams. Happiness is something that's beyond it. I honestly believe that getting the right food in your mind, getting your heart, mind, and spirit in a right place trumps fulfilling your dreams.

So, I'm going to say the opposite. Fulfilling your dreams will not fulfill your dreams. Learn to be content and joyful in the journey, wherever you are, and in whatever you are doing. Joy is not an ongoing sense of ecstasy; it's a contentment in the journey.

Also, I'd say that if your dream is based around you making a lot of money, I guarantee it won't make you happy. I've had all the things that I thought you were supposed to have. It didn't make me happy, it actually caused me more stress. Every single square foot of your big house that you have is decaying at every moment. It requires upkeep, maintenance. It's rotting before your very eyes.

Do you want to spend your life maintaining your stuff, or do you want to live? So, there you go, that's a lot of rambling, but these are the things that I've been learning the hard way over the last few years. This is actually part of the reason why we are doing this RV thing. Someone once said to me, "You know you've only got eighteen summers with your kids." That means I've only got six summers left with my kids. Six summers left to train them before they go off to school, or college, or leave home, or whatever. So, we are gonna go out and live life right now, teach them and love them, broaden their minds, and give 'em God's perspective.

**WAYNE:** So good. Wow, thank you so much for taking the time to talk. What you are saying about having joy in the journey is so true. I don't know if this book I'm working on is meant to be read by 200, 500, 3,000, or 30,000 people. All of that is in God's hands.

I'm just so glad that I get to share these stories. Chatting with Ainslie reminded me that the outcome isn't actually the goal. The goal is to enjoy the journey with those I love and to keep growing, too. Relieving myself of the pressure to succeed just for the sake of success, and being present in every moment—that's something I want to be brave enough to jump into.

# DENNIS

"Let's see, we are cycling from San Diego, California, to the Florida coast.
I think we are on day number thirty-one so far."

That's all I got—*Dennis*—I didn't get his last name.

A few months ago, I was tent camping with my family in Fredericksburg, Texas. We were truly roughing it. I mean, yeah, we brought extensions cords and my laptop and some movies. A blow-up mattress. Stuffed animals. Bikes. It was like home away from home and super fun.

One afternoon, when we returned to our campsite after a fun hike up Enchanted Rock, we had some visitors moving in next door. There were about twelve senior citizens and two or three folks in their twenties, and they were all on bicycles. They looked pretty serious. I mean, these folks had only the bare minimum with them on these bikes. But they each had a small, single-person tent, cooking equipment, and a change of clothes. This was an amazing scene.

I walked over to them to say hi and met Dennis, and our conversation from that day follows.

WAYNE: Hi, there! What are you folks up to? You guys look like you've been on quite a journey!

DENNIS: Yes, indeed. Let's see, we are cycling from San Diego, California, to the Florida coast. I think we are on day number thirty-one so far.

WAYNE: That's amazing! What a cool thing to do. How much longer will it take you guys, you think?

DENNIS: I think we have about thirty days to go.

WAYNE: If you don't mind me asking, how old are you?

DENNIS: *[laughing]* Age is just a number. But, yeah, I'm seventy. By the way, your two little girls over there sure are cute. Just wait until they are like thirteen or fourteen. You'll be sitting on a hard bleacher somewhere watching them play volleyball or softball or something. Enjoy the ride.

WAYNE: Will do. You too, Dennis!

Awesome.

# CONNOR KETCHUM

> "I walked out into the river carrying the two empty bladders, and
> I could see a mama bear feeding her cubs. Normally, this type of
> scene would encourage me, but I just wanted to die for some reason.
> Mentally and physically at the end, I walked out into the middle of
> this river. I just stood there weeping, and really just throwing myself
> a pity party. I was ready to give up and throw in the towel."

Last year I flew to Colorado to attend the Wild at Heart Boot Camp, a men's conference put on by John Eldredge and Wild at Heart. It's an incredible and intense weekend with four hundred and fifty guys. Thousands apply each year, and it's basically a lottery system to see who gets in. This event is a weekend deal where men go to be real with each other, to be real with God, and to hunt down wholeheartedness. I felt blessed to be there. The camp is held in the mountains of Colorado at approximately nine thousand feet. For this Houston boy, it was pretty mind-blowing.

Since I was there by myself, as opposed to being with a group, at each meal I'd end up sitting with a new bunch of guys. At the conference, the men are all served in a big dining hall of a rustic camp. There were guys from all over the United States and some from abroad. Basically, every single meal was a new adventure; you just never knew who you'd meet, what their story was, and what stories would be shared.

One of the guys I was fortunate enough to connect with was Connor Ketchum. At one of the meals we were sitting next to each other and began to chat.

**WAYNE:** What do you do for work, Connor?

**CONNOR:** I'm a fishing and trip guide in Alaska four months of the year, in some of the most unreal and remote places of creation. The rest of the year, I'm in Denver.

**WAYNE:** Bro. A guide in Alaska? Wait, how old are you? *(This guy looked pretty young for such craziness!)*

**CONNOR:** I'm twenty-five.

**WAYNE:** I'm trying to think of what I was doing when I was twenty-five, and I sure wasn't doing anything on the scale of leading adventurous trips in the wilderness.

We chatted quite a bit that day, and over the weekend. Connor and I stayed in touch all this year, and when I began putting this book together, I just knew I needed to pick his brain about what he was up to.

**WAYNE:** Man, tell me your story. How in the world does a guy end up doing what you're doing? What was the road that took you there? How did your love of the wild places begin?

**CONNOR:** My first strong memory of anything to do with nature is when I was very young. I was about four or five years old, and my dad took me and a few of his friends from work on a short in-town hike, basically to a park in Atlanta. My dad was a CPA and they were talking work stuff, and I was running around by this creek. I just remember being so thrilled to be out there. The story goes that I yelled, "Dad!" and they turned around to see me caught up in a tree, buck naked, screaming, "I'm alive!"

**WAYNE:** Whoa. Nice!

**CONNOR:** I guess they knew they had a wild child on their hands. Once my parents had to call the police to get me down from another tree I was stuck in. Evidently, I was all the way at the top. I thought that there was no point in climbing a tree if I wasn't gonna go to the top, y'know?

My dad cultivated that wild spirit in me. When I was fifteen, my dad did a "coming to manhood" ceremony, spoke into my life, and even gave me a shotgun. Also, that same year I went with some of my friends and some of Dad's friends to climb one of the 14K mountain peaks of Colorado. My strongest encouraging memory is that I was invited into the campfire talk. In that moment, I basically became just one of the guys. I have a great photo from that trip where me and my dad got caught in a crazy sleet storm, and we were just hunkered down riding it out, and I remember feeling that feeling again, "I am alive!"

My high school years were kind of troubled for some reason. A lot of dark moments, unhealthy relationships, things sucking the life out of me, even tension in my own family. At one point, I even attempted suicide; it was very hard on me and my family. I didn't want to go to college. In my town, if you didn't go to college, well, you were an unspoken failure.

A youth minister took me under his wing and literally saved my life. He supported me and encouraged me through that time. It turned my life around. I ended up deciding to go to a Bible College that was in Canada. I used my car savings money to pay for it. Then I went off to the University of Arkansas to study Business. But really, my sole purpose was to share light in dark places.

While in college, I had a few opportunities to go on some guided fly fishing trips. Not only did I love being in the wild again, but I started seeing how much it made me feel alive to just facilitate conversations with people. All of a sudden, I'm out in the woods with these high-profile people—CEOs and VPs of big companies—and I'm realizing we are all the same. Out in the wilderness, titles don't really matter anymore.

Next thing I knew, I had gotten connected with a mom-and-pop outfit in Alaska, and after I graduated from college, I was off to Alaska. I loved the risk taking. It became this dream coming to life, to actually create space for people to get uncomfortable. In the outdoors, people get real with each other pretty quickly.

Just as things were starting to go really well, life threw me a huge curve ball. I was going to propose to my girlfriend at the lodge where I was working. Literally, on my birthday, I received a call from the outfit owner saying he was selling the lodge and leaving the business. Not only would I lose this picture-perfect moment I had planned, to ask her to marry me out there, but it hit me that my professional dream had now been yanked from me. I remember literally crying and falling in my dad's arms. I had no idea what was next for me.

Side note, I could totally relate to what Connor was sharing with me. Have you ever been at such a spot on your journey? I imagine that you have. We are cruising along, even running full throttle into the dream we are living out, and, all of a sudden, bam! There goes the rug under our feet. There's the unexpected twist, diagnosis, financial setback, that we didn't see coming.

You're not alone, my friend. Every single person that I connected with this year has been in this spot before and understands the reality that they'll be there again. The thing is deciding that this dip in the story will not define how the story ends.

Connor went on to say that the season that followed was one of waiting. Being patient. I don't know about you, but I'm not a big fan of being patient. But, oh, what we might learn in the waiting.

A year later, Connor found himself on a float plane in the middle of the Alaskan wilderness, leading a trip for a new company. His dream was becoming a reality. He was now employed by an outfitter. Weekly, during the summer months, he and his crew are dropped off via plane with a boat, tents, food, and a "good luck" wave. Six days and fifty miles of river later, the teams reach their destination.

**CONNOR:** I can't believe how amazing these experiences have been. To be able to take teams of people out into the wild and allow them to experience things they never imagined. I'm talking about doctors and financial advisors getting dirt under their fingernails, and truly experiencing the wild and God's creation; it's incredible. It's both exhausting, and incredible.

About two years ago, I had an unreal moment. Week after week, teams of people are coming in, and I do love it, but I found out that everyone has a limit of how much they can do without a break. After six straight weeks, I was in the middle of a trip leading some folks and I realized I was physically, emotionally, and spiritually exhausted. On this trip, I woke up one morning and realized I had forgotten to hang the water filtration bags the night before. This is my typical routine so we can all have water the next day. That day it was about forty degrees, and we were in the middle of nowhere. It was raining like crazy, with winds blowing thirty miles per hour, and I felt this was the last straw for my heart. I walked out into the river carrying the two empty bladders, and I could see a mama bear feeding her cubs. Normally, this type of scene would encourage me, but I just wanted to die for some reason. Mentally and physically at the end, I walked out into the middle of this river. I just stood there weeping, and really just throwing myself a pity party. I was ready to give up and throw in the towel. But I knew I had this group of guys I had to get safely back to civilization.

I filled the water bladders, walked back to camp, and, soaking wet, decided I needed something warm to drink to help revive me. I'd been drinking these Good Earth teas that summer; I love the taste, but they also have these cool quotes on the tea bags. I know this sounds a little crazy, but I had this prophetic and powerful moment out there and felt like God was reminding me of what it was I was doing out there. This tea bag I opened said "You cannot lead where you do not go."

I started weeping again as I realized, wow—I was out there not willing to go where I was taking these people. I wasn't allowing myself to get to my own breaking point, or my own point of discomfort, so that I might hear and see clearly what's truly important. Man, this changed the game for me. I feel like it's totally applicable to entrepreneurs and risk-takers. I think for people who want to launch out, do these radical things, it's a great reminder. You can't ask people to go where you aren't willing to go yourself.

That experience not only helped me to finish strong that summer, but it launched me into a full-time career with this thing. I had to get back to that "I'm alive" moment I'd had as a kid. I was reminded that, for me, the less "safe" I am by the world's standards, the more I can hear God's voice and direction in my life.

WAYNE: Incredible, bro. Thank you for sharing this. Okay, last question: What do you think is the biggest "life sucker" to a dream chaser out there?

CONNOR: Fear of approval. I know it sounds a little cliché, but, for real. Fear of people's approval can and will literally paralyze you. It can stop you in your tracks—stop you from doing and being who you were created to be. It will mute you. Don't compare yourself to other people, period. Silence all those voices, and instead of saying, "What if?" say "Why not?"

Over the past year Connor has sent me several incredible photos he has taken while in Alaska. After he found out that I was a painter, he sent a few over for me to consider using for reference photographs. One in particular was an incredible shot of two bears near a river. One was perched on top of a big rock looking down into the water, about ready to pounce on some fish. The other bear was standing next to him, trying to decide his plan of attack. I did a painting of this image, and called it "Brunch."

I actually sent a large print of this to John Eldredge while I was trying to convince him to let me interview him. You'll see later in this book that not only did he say yes to the interview, but he also said, "Pretty risky sending artwork."

True! But it pays to be brave.

## SOME THINGS TO KICK AROUND

1. Which of these interviews have stuck out to you the most thus far?

2. Is there an area of doubt that you feel like you need to defeat?

3. Is there a vision or a dream that you are ready to make a jump into?

## chapter four
# MERAKI

"Success is no accident. It is hard work, perseverance, learning, studying, sacrifice, and most of all, love of what you are doing."[11]

—Pele

**MERAKI** - {v.} or {adv.} A modern Greek word, derived from the Turkish "merak." A labor of love, to do something with pleasure, applied to tasks, usually creative or artistic tasks, but can be applied to any task at all. Meraki means to do something with passion, with absolute devotion, with undivided attention. Meraki is also used to describe what happens when you leave a piece of yourself (your soul, creativity, or love) in your work. When you love doing something so much that you put something of yourself into it.[12]

I don't know about you, but I can tell. I can tell when someone has put their entire self into it. I can tell when someone has just phoned it in. Boy, does it show.

Music, art, or a meal, I can tell when someone has taken the time to lovingly, carefully, and with all their heart, bring themselves fully to the work.

We were recently in Ruidoso, New Mexico. While my girls were running around having fun at a little cabin there, I found myself getting 3.4 minutes to have a quiet space. I was lying facedown on a bed, sprawled out, exhausted from a morning hike we had all gone on. I opened my eyes and noticed this wooden end table that sat next to the bed. It wasn't just an end table; it was a piece of artwork. It was a mission-style piece of furniture that had been hand made. I blinked a few times and started really studying it. This thing has tongue and groove fittings. There were no nails. Whoa. I was blown away by all the intricate details that went into this piece.

Then I noticed my keys, rings, and cell phone that were sitting on top of it. They had been there for the past couple days, and I had never once stopped to notice this end table. I tried to imagine who the woodworker was who'd made this. Was it done in the 1950s? The 40s? Had she spent weeks on this? Was she rattling the cages of the woodworking world since it was since it was an all-guys profession? Had it been done by an elderly man who'd spent his retirement lovingly working on such a craft? Whoever it had been, I could tell they'd derived some serious joy from working on this piece. This was not a cookie-cutter, cheaply made production table. A craftsperson put their heart into it, whether it would be appreciated or not.

I realized I don't often just stop and notice much of what people are putting their whole selves into. But when I do stop, I notice that something comes alive in me. I heard a cool quote one time by famous painter Georgia O'Keeffe. She was asked what inspired her to start doing such huge, oversized flower paintings, and she said, "When you take a flower in your hand and really look at it, it's your world for the moment. I want to give that world to someone else. Most people in the city rush around, so they have no time to look at a flower. I want them to see it whether they want to or not."[13]

There's something deep in the programming of my heart that yearns to give my all, my very best. Forget leaving a hint of my fingerprints on it; I want to leave part of my very soul in what I am working on. So, I truly enjoyed this next set of interviews with people who are doing the same and who are living out meraki. I hope you're encouraged.

# RAYMOND TURNER

> "Yeah, when I saw that word 'meraki,' it struck me. To put so much of myself into something that I leave part of my soul in it, has become something that I can't not do. I can't not put all of myself into the work."

Raymond Turner was the first person to ever mention this word "meraki" to me. I've known Raymond for over twenty years and am so thankful to call him my friend. I'm beyond blessed to be able to share his story and heart with you. For several years, "RayRay" (as I lovingly call him), or "Ray2," played drums with me. Whether at a small camp in the middle of nowhere, or at a large event with thousands of kids, or in the studio recording, Raymond always brought his best. Meraki.

Today, Raymond heads up an amazing recording studio called "Sparklefly." The studio is unique. Why? Because it is located inside of Cook Children's Medical Center in Dallas, Texas.

Sparklefly is a professional, state of the art, recording space. What makes this studio so very special is that Raymond uses it to help children who are battling illness write and record their own songs. These are beautiful gifts of love, not only to the families, but also for encouraging and empowering these children and young people. Some of the work Raymond does involves taking the heartbeats of little ones in the NICU unit. He lovingly takes their heartbeat and puts music to it for their family. Some of these children are either premature, battling to survive, or have already passed away. My goodness.

Beautiful and amazing.

I knew when putting this book project together that RayRay had to be a part of it. What does it really look like to put all of yourself fully into your work? Calling, loss, renewal, music, and passing on the blessing are all part of his story. What a joy and privilege to chat with him on the phone and share his heart with you.

**WAYNE:** Man! Tell us your story. I know when you were a kid, you got in trouble in school for tapping your desk over and over. The drummer in you was already trying to come out.

**RAYMOND:** *[laughs]* Yes! As a kid, growing up, I loved music but was never any good at it. But, I remember, in seventh grade I was sitting there tapping and tapping on my desk. My English teacher got so mad and finally said, "If you're going to keep doing that, maybe you need to go down the hall and join the band." And so I did. I remember the first time I walked into the huge band hall. I just had this overwhelming feeling that this was home, and that I'd be doing this for the rest of my life.

**WAYNE:** I need to find that English teacher and thank her!

**RAYMOND:** So, yeah, I started plugging into band, then I got something amazing—a small Casio keyboard. I grew up with my grandma, and she was so supportive. I would just sit around and make things up. I had no idea what I was doing, I just knew I loved making music. It was really strange, any time I would play, or make up things, it would feel as if someone somewhere was listening to me. Looking back now, it's wild. I would ask my teachers for pictures of different places around the world. I'd set these images up in front of my keyboard and just try and play music that matched how the picture felt. This one book had pictures of castles and mountains, all kinds of places. I would try and play chords or sounds that would take me there. Without really knowing it, I was learning how major and minor chords make you feel. From then till now, I try to paint what I feel with music.

I continued pursuing music through college. One of my professors in particular helped to try and draw things out of me. People thought I was extroverted, but really, I was trying to cover up some deficiencies I felt on the inside. I was really an introvert. So, this professor tried to pull a lot of that out of me. I had gotten to where I could read music, and I was playing the right notes, but I was struggling to pull things from a real place inside of me, really getting to the heart of who I was. And, I will say this, playing music with you, Wayne, brought out a whole lot more than you realize.

**WAYNE:** Uh oh! What did I do?

70

**RAYMOND:** I'm not sure if I've told you about this, but when I started playing with you, I was really into jazz, and I tried to keep everything inside the lines. And playing with you, I remember you saying things like, "Play out!" and I was a little resistant at first. I was thinking, *Hey, I'm playing, I'm just not gonna go crazy.* I'll never forget, we were at some event with like 1,400 kids, and it was this freeing moment when you turned around and screamed, "Drum solo!"

**WAYNE:** Oh my gosh!

**RAYMOND:** My whole body broke out into a sweat and hives, and I was like, okay, I can't be this playing-everything-right, playing-by-the-rules-type drummer. I had to let everything go! The kids were bouncing, jumping to the beat, and I just thought I have to go for it. And, you know, that was actually a breakthrough moment in my life, musically. Realizing I can let go, and impact people in that way.

**WAYNE:** I think I should have given you a little notice, though! I still have no idea what I'm really doing, but probably less so back then. I remember being in the studio with y'all and not even knowing the chord names or key signatures of my songs. I'd just say, "It goes like this, and this, and then, this." Then one of you guys would translate for the rest of the band in the Nashville number system chording . . . 6, 4, 1. And I remember saying, "Hey, I don't need your phone number, I just need you, so play the song!" So silly. So, after college for you, then what?

**RAYMOND:** I started working with different musicians, playing in different churches, different styles. It not only broadened my mind as a musician, but I started learning how it was really more about relationships. So many amazing connections.

**WAYNE:** Okay. Now, fast-forward to where you are now. How did this opportunity come about for you? When you heard about it, did you think this was a perfect fit for you, or did you walk slowly through that door?

**RAYMOND:** Honestly, before this opportunity came about, I was in a rough place. I was kind of angry with God, if I'm honest. I guess the best way to put it is I felt frustrated about where I was in life and in my calling. It was at the point where I was just about to sell all my recording equipment. I was starting to feel like I might even be done with music. When we found out that Cook Children's in Dallas was building a studio and looking for someone to head it up, I just thought, *That's an odd combination, a recording studio inside a hospital.* It struck something with my heart, so I went ahead and applied. I remember my wife Maria literally said, "We're moving." Whoa, hold up. She started packing up things little by little. I'm looking at her like she's crazy! I did a phone interview, and honestly, after that I thought there was no way this would work out. I felt even more depressed about things. I had put my heart into so many things before this, only to see them stripped away. I sure didn't want to go through that again.

**WAYNE:** There are so many hills and valleys in people's lives. From the outside, folks might have never guessed you were dealing with doubts like that.

**RAYMOND:** Totally. You know, even after going up there to do the in-person interview, I remember thinking God was just setting me up for another disappointment, another fall. I thought, *I'm done with music.* That night I was lying in bed, and I felt as if God asked me, "What do you want?" It took me by surprise. Why would God ask me that? I said, "Lord, this feels like the most amazing thing, and what you've created me to do, and, yes, I want this." It was a few days later that they called and offered me the position. It happened so fast. And even now, I've told the administration there that when I step into that place each day, I feel like I'm stepping literally into what God created me to do.

**WAYNE:** So powerful. Tell me about the heartbeat recordings that you guys do.

**RAYMOND:** It's very special. We take the heartbeats of terminally ill infants and children, and put music on top of it as a gift to the family. The doctors bring this recording to me, the precious heartbeat of a little one who is either about to pass away or has just passed recently. I just sit there alone listening to the heartbeat of this little baby. It's so powerful and such an honor. We then build a song on top of that heartbeat. Sometimes the heartbeat is steady, sometimes it has irregularities. I sit with the family and get their input on it as well. Sometimes, it's a song that has been meaningful to them. Next, we rearrange that song to fit the tempo of that heartbeat. We often build in certain sounds or instruments that the child may have liked. What a joy and blessing to help create something meaningful for them, that they can hold onto for the rest of their lives.

**WAYNE:** That is so special, man. It's beyond words really what you are putting your heart and hand to for these precious families.

**RAYMOND:** I was doing a TV interview one time, and she was asking about the heartbeat recordings that we do. We talked about the process. And toward the end of the interview I remember she just tossed out one last question. She asked, "Why do you do this?" It was a surreal moment. I think I knew the answer to that, but I had never pulled it out; I'd kept it stored away. I just looked at her, and I started crying. Finally, I said, "You know, it's interesting how God is a redeemer. We sing these songs about that, but He really is a redeemer." I shared with her how we lost our first child. Five months into our pregnancy, we went for the ultrasound. The one thing that you go there for, to hear your child's heartbeat, we left not having heard that sound. I told her, "What I wasn't able to have, God has redeemed so that is exactly what I am able to give back to these parents. God prepared me for these moments, unknowingly.

**WAYNE:** And you named the studio Sparklefly Studio. Tell me about the name.

**RAYMOND:** The name came about after being here a year. Anytime I name something, or write a mission statement, I give it some time to see what I'm actually doing. It's easy to throw up a name, but I wanted it to come out of what we were doing here. One of the other main things I do here is to song-write with students and youth who are going through treatments of some kind. If you were to hear what some of them are going through, my mind is continually blown by these kids. These kids are not only super talented, but their faith, their belief in God is so inspiring. Despite if they were healed or not, the faith I kept seeing was unshakable. Some of them facing terminal diagnosis, some treatable, some with bullying in the midst of all they are facing . . . I kept looking at the darkness in the backdrop of their lives, and they just light up the place. I kept thinking of fireflies. You know, fireflies are this anomaly. You don't have to plug them in. They are captivating, but you only see them at night, or in the twilight. You can sit for hours and be mesmerized because they really don't make sense. These kids are the fireflies. They are the ones who are lighting up the darkness they are going through. The other element of it is the sparks that they bring. We want to take those embers, we breathe on them, but our prayer is that God lights those things up. So that's where that came out of. I realized a year and half into it, this was the vision for what we were doing.

**WAYNE:** I also understand that the studio setup is insanely cool and was donated by an up and coming country musician.

**RAYMOND:** *[laughs]* Yes. Garth Brooks had a huge part in making it a reality. He is part of an organization called TeamMates, and they basically financially helped make it happen. In fact, his audio engineer came and laid out the power grid of the place and did the entire design. The audio console, outboard gear, guitars— all of it was donated. Anything you would find at any other major studio is here.

**WAYNE:** Let's talk about meraki. You know, it's your fault that there's an entire chapter here dedicated to this. You were the one who introduced me to the word. Because some people are okay to just do a job they don't like for all of their days, just to get a paycheck. And then, for whatever reason, there are other people, who, even if they weren't being paid, would still be putting their whole heart into something. They would probably still be putting chords and music over a child's heartbeat, because it makes them come alive. Tell me how you first heard of "meraki" and your thoughts on it.

**RAYMOND:** A few years ago, I came across it on this "vocabulary word of the day" thing. At first I thought it was a Japanese word. As I started looking into the meaning of it, I was stunned. The word encapsulated not only what I hope to do with my life, from day to day, but also in everything I put my hand to. If I'm writing a song with a patient, we are all in. We're gonna extract the meaning from this song. Now the students know that when they come in to record something, it's not a quick rushed process. It's not like, "Okay great, good take. We are done." It's a four- to five-hour process. Not only are we there to record a great vocal performance, but we're talking with them throughout the process. What are you thinking about? Why did you write it? That vocal inflection needs to sound the way the lyric is describing how you feel. And to your point, the things I've done in my life, either where I wasn't paid, or paid very little, I always put more into it than anyone expected. So, yeah, when I saw that word "meraki," it struck me. To put so much of myself into something that I leave part of my soul in it, has become something that I can't not do. I can't not put all of myself into the work.

I feel that God has put such a desire within me for excellence—the passion to give my all. And it's not so much about my name being remembered. My prayer my whole life has been for God to please leave something of His residue on the work I'm doing. That's why whether it's a heartbeat, or sitting with a patient working on a song, I want to give my very best.

**WAYNE:** As long as I've known you, you've been the type of person that gives 100 percent to whatever you put your hand to.

**RAYMOND:** You know, my grandmother who raised me would tell me the story of how I was born. The fact is that I, too, was born premature. In fact, I weighed barely two pounds when I was born. She talked about the fragility of all that. She said that the doctors didn't even think I was going to make it, or, if I did, I might be a vegetable. When she would share those stories, it was like something she was just recalling. That did something powerful for me growing up. I would see some of my friends going off the rails, or making bad decisions. But that story, *my* story, impressed on me the fact that I'm literally blessed to still be here, and I can't screw this up. God brought me through all this and has purpose for my life. I think that's why I want to live with such gratefulness and give my all to everything. Whatever you have for me, Lord, I'm all in.

**WAYNE:** What's been one of the highlights for you thus far in this Sparklefly Studio work?

**RAYMOND:** One of the greatest things so far has been a young man named Randon. When he came into the hospital at ten years old, he mentioned that he loved to sing. Over these past couple years, we worked together, and we recorded him singing a tune called "Rise Up." It was shared online, and people keep sharing it. It was the biggest joy to call them the other day and say, "There are over 100,000 views of you singing!" His heart was so huge to just want to sing for other kids at the hospital. It thrilled me beyond belief to know that so many people have been blessed by his voice. It's like the loaves and fishes story in the Bible, where Jesus could have just said "poof" and fed everyone. But he gave the loaves and fishes to the disciples, and he told them to pass it out. So, they were a part of holding and seeing it happen. They could see what was in the basket, but as they were passing it out, its coming through their hands. To be able to help give him voice, to help usher that along, it's mind-blowing. That's what I love, seeing that happen.

**WAYNE:** Okay, last question, and I'm hitting most people with this question, so I'm sorry in advance. What would forty-six-year-old Raymond tell twenty-year-old Raymond?

**RAYMOND:** Stay on your assignment. The things that you're going to go through will all shape you, they won't break you. Stay on the course. Keep your heart and stay on assignment. Don't let anything steal your heart or steal your passion. I think, even then, twenty-year-old Raymond had an assignment, and things and people get in the way, well-meaning people, even church people. Don't lose the passion to be curious. Don't lose the wonder of things. We are born with curiosity and creativity, and sometimes we lose it along the way. Sometimes the things that we think were meant to feed us can devour us if we're not careful. So, twenty-year-old Raymond, stay the course, stay on your assignment. It took me a while to get back to my first love. Don't allow people to try and tell you who you are in the process.

**WAYNE:** Dude, thank you so much. You are inspiring, man.

**RAYMOND:** Hey, I also want to thank you for that "Colored Leaves" painting you did, based on Jeremiah 17:7. I ordered a couple of those because I want to put that in the vocal booth at the studio. Because that's been my prayer for the songs that those kids do, that the kids who need healing would receive that through the song. Not only the ones who are singing them, but those songs would be healing leaves for people. Whether it be in the hospital, the community, or the world at large.

# TOTO

When I turned fifty, I talked my wife into letting me go see one of the greatest bands ever, Toto! And yes, I paid extra for the meet and greet, soundcheck party, front row experience. For real. They were in town the week of my birthday for Pete's sake! For some of you who have "kinda" heard of them, it's probably because of songs like "Africa" and "Rosanna," from the 80s.

For the serious musician who may be reading this, you already know that these guys were basically the top studio musicians in LA for more than twenty years. Between them, they have played on over five thousand albums, respectfully. Michael Jackson's *Thriller* album was basically the band Toto on most instruments. Toto has recorded fourteen records, sold over 44 million albums, and have won multiple Grammys.[14]

For me on that day in August, I was like a little kid. I headed to the Woodlands Amphitheater several hours before the show. When they let us VIP folks into the front gates, I was pumped. There were eighty-eight people in the front section of this outdoor venue that seats thousands of people. The Toto guys were already on stage getting sound check rolling. If you could have seen my face, it was probably hilarious. There was a continual smile was on my face for that entire time. Steve Lukather on guitar, David Paich on piano, Steve Porcaro on keys, Joseph Williams on vocals—I mean, are you kidding me? Again, no offense taken here for those of you saying, "Who are these people?" But hang with me for a second, and I'll make my point.

They did some Q&A, played through a few sound check things, cracked some jokes, and it was amazing. It sounded crazy incredible, and it was wild to be there with eighty-eight other people in this huge venue watching this in person. But, the part that really got my attention was this. Toward the end of the sound check they were practicing this one tune in particular. When they finished, Lukather said, "Lets run the end of that tune again, but really accent that snare hit coming into the last measure." They did the ending again. Then Paich offered a slight correction on how the band was needing to tighten up. They did the ending again. Then they ran the ending again. After the fourth time, you could tell they couldn't care less who the eighty-eight people were standing there. The simple truth was, they wanted to *nail* that ending in the show later. I stood there thinking, *This is like my Wednesday night rehearsals at church!*

I watched them as they worked it a few more times, and suddenly it hit me. There's a reason these guys have made such an impact on the music scene for over four decades. They truly care about their craft. They put their heart and soul into every note they play. Every melody, arrangement, decision about dynamics, and key change, all of it. It all matters. These guys were not there that night in Houston just to make a paycheck, they were there to give their very best for their fans. They were putting their whole selves into it. Then they took a break, and I was able to fly a drone with Joseph Williams, which was crazy.

Meraki.

About an hour later, as the doors opened, thousands of people started pouring in. Toto hadn't played live in Houston in years, so their fans came out that night like crazy. As twilight fell and the show started, the smile on my face was still there. They played hit after hit, followed by newer tunes, followed by crazy instrumental feats that I could never aspire to achieve.

I left that night pretty much blown away. I was reminded that I want to give my all in whatever I put my hand to. That night, I was inspired to keep striving after this. I want to live out this meraki thing.

Oh, by the way, they nailed the ending.

# JUSTIN GERARD

> "Forget the hashtags. Do the art, and they will come. It seems like aspiring artists come to me all the time looking for some sort of secret shortcut to success. There is no such thing. It's really about daily practice. I call it 'knuckle pushups' for the brain."

Justin Gerard is an illustrator and painter based in Georgia. He has illustrated tons of books. I've been a huge fan for years. His illustrations of Tolkien stories will blow your mind. If you weren't nervous about a dragon flying overhead before, you will be now. Or if you couldn't quite imagine what a huge battle looks like between thousands of dwarfs and orcs, his imagination and creativity can get you there.

I was beyond thrilled to get to connect with him over coffee in Canton, Georgia. I shared a bit about this word "meraki" that we are unpacking here. (And I had something up my sleeve for the end of the interview.)

**WAYNE:** How did you first get into drawing?

**JUSTIN:** From the moment I first learned that crayons were meant for coloring and not for eating, I've been drawing. I grew up loving it, and with a huge curiosity about how to capture the beauty of the creatures of the world. There was a book I read when I was young called *Drawing Animals* and it totally blew my mind.

**WAYNE:** It's apparent in your work that you put your whole self in the process.

**JUSTIN:** My wife, Annie Stegg, is a full-time painter as well. I guess it's a bit unusual that we are both artists. Literally, we are both so passionate about our work that we panic on a daily basis about how to capture our shadows better.

**WAYNE:** That is totally something an artist would say. Well, it sure shows how much you love the work, and we can all see how you put yourself into it. I can also tell you have a love for classic literature. Is this where some of this inspiration comes from?

**JUSTIN:** For sure. I love the works of J.R.R. Tolkien and C.S. Lewis, and they are still inspiring my work today. I got to do a little pre-production work on *The Hobbit* films a few years ago, and it was amazing.

**WAYNE:** What advice would you give to artists out there who are trying to make a go at doing art for a living?

**JUSTIN:** Forget the hashtags. Do the art, and they will come. It seems like aspiring artists come to me all the time looking for some sort of secret shortcut to success. There is no such thing. It's really about daily practice. I call it "knuckle pushups for the brain." Like I said before, I'm literally always trying to improve at light and shadows.

**WAYNE:** It seems like in the art world, like everything else, things change quickly. I guess you have to learn to adapt or you're in trouble. I know in the course of my sixteen years doing music for a living, I saw the music industry evolve in front of my very eyes. I went from selling my first album on a cassette in 1995 to selling CDs to selling songs for one dollar on iTunes to now streaming online, where basically no one is "buying" your music. How have you seen things change with technology over your career?

**JUSTIN:** Yep, even as short as ten years ago, it was a totally different world in the art community. Social media has changed things in huge ways. But, basically, at this point I kind of have what I call the five pillars of my career: 1) Freelance work 2) Selling my original pieces 3) My online store 4) Patreon (which is basically a subscription based service where people get art monthly from me) and 5) Kickstarter. All of this stuff helps me to creatively find ways to reach enough people so that I can keep doing what I love. I do feel I'm pretty much the luckiest guy in the world, who just happened to be born at a time in history where I can do art and pursue this passion full time.

As we were wrapping up our time together, I said, "Okay, I have one last thing to ask you, and feel free to say no. At this he looked a little nervous. Especially as I pulled out of my backpack a large drawing pad and some pencils.

I said, "Several years ago I bought a very small illustration on Ebay from comic artist John Byrne. (Yes, super geek moment right now.) It was called "Thirty-second Batman." It was a quick loose sketch, and I love it. Again, feel no pressure to say yes, but would you consider drawing me a "Three-minute Dragon"?

He was kind and agreed.

What was actually amazing was, from the second that he took the art pad from me and started looking through my pencils to see what the options were, his countenance changed. He transformed in front of my eyes. He instantly went from a guy who was being kind enough to sit through an interview with some guy from Texas, talking about all this, to a passionate and gifted artist who is on fire about his craft.

His hand was darting back and forth across the page as he smiled and began sharing, "When I start, I always start super loosely, so that you can get the composition right within the space." He was in his zone, his space, and within sixty seconds, I could see a very rough layout of a dragon who didn't look too pleased. Most of the drawing was loose and blurry. Then he grabbed a technical pencil and started detailing the face.

"You don't want the entire image of whatever you are working on to be in focus. The human eye doesn't even work like that. I just give enough information so the onlooker sees what's happening and your brain fills in all the details."

I'm sure at this point to anyone walking by us sitting in this coffeeshop, that I looked like a twelve-year-old kid whose eyes were open wide, as if I'd just found the open door into Narnia for this guy.

"This is totally rocking my world," I said as he kept working and chatting while he drew. These three minutes were the highlight of my time with him.

Next thing I knew, he said, "Here you go." He signed the bottom, and then added, "Oh, one second, there needs to be just a little bit of smoke coming up from his nostrils right here."

And there it was, my own personal "Three-minute Dragon."

I am currently at my family's little cabin typing, typing, typing. The treehouse is still standing, so that's a win. As I sit here in this little sixteen by sixteen cabin, lots of memories from these interviews are crashing into me. I believe that when we encounter people who fully put themselves into their work, it leaves a mark on us. And I believe when we live our lives this way, there is a deep joy that comes from it. I hope that these stories are inspiring you to be a person who lives meraki in whatever you put your hand to.

My family came today to visit me here for a bit while I'm working on this, and my sweet Elliott, after reading this over my shoulder said, "Can I type something?"

"Of course," I said.

She typed this, and I think it is pretty much the truth:

I love to draw so much
It is so fun
—Elliott

## BRANDI LISENBE

Brandi cuts my hair y'all.

She is an entrepreneur who is going for it. She is the owner of Do or Dye in the Heights of Houston, Texas. One day she said something pretty amazing. I just *had* to include it in here. One day, while she was snipping away, somehow the discussion came to coffee.

Brandi said, "I don't like lukewarm, I want my coffee either super hot, or iced and really cold. Why would you want it room temperature?"

C'mon, that'll preach.

As I drove home that day, her words were bouncing around in my heart and head. Not to mention that Jesus said the exact same thing about our spiritual lives. I think the same thing applies to our creative lives, and everything else for that matter.

Why not completely go for it? Meraki is never lukewarm.

# DAVID McCLISTER

"We were with him doing a shoot for an album cover, and I was just working away, staying focused. We did a few test shots with a polaroid type camera. And I remember laying the shots out on the ground, and it really hit me, I was like, 'Holy cow, that's Eric Clapton! He did stuff with the Beatles!' I had to compose myself and get back to it. But it was pretty awesome."

David McClister has captured in photograph and on film some of the greatest musicians of our time. From Miranda Lambert to Dolly Parton, Willie Nelson to Taylor Swift, Leon Bridges to Robert Plant, Sheryl Crowe to Kings of Leon to The Band Perry. The list is somewhat endless. He has a unique thing about capturing them on film in a way that seems timeless. If you were to scroll through his images, most of which are in black and white, you would get the feeling that you're not exactly sure what year the photos were taken. He has done work for *Rolling Stone* magazine, *TIME* magazine, *Billboard* magazine, and tons more.

I first connected with David when I was trying to track down who the photographer was on a Willie Nelson image that I was painting. Once I found him, I naturally checked out his other work. Wow, the long list of people who he has worked with is ridiculous. More importantly, I was struck by his ability to capture these folks in such every-day and human ways. I have worked with some photographers before, and there are tons of great ones out there. I know how hard it must be to get your subject to feel relaxed enough so that the perfect image can be snapped, one that really reflects who they are as an individual and artist.

David and I connected in Nashville for a brief chat over some coffee.

**WAYNE:** How did you get into photography?

**DAVID:** When I was in high school, my dad got me a Canon camera. (I was a skater; I was not good, by the way.) So, I played around with it. Honestly, at first I was just taking skater pics, having fun with it. Then later in life, I got into music and bands, and I just started taking pics of local bands. These were friends of mine, out playing live. Little did I know that getting that camera back then would change my life so much.

**WAYNE:** You have shot such a wide range of people, such amazing artists. One thing I noticed is that people seem so relaxed and personable. How do you pull that off?

**DAVID:** I recently did a shoot with Lucas Nelson (Willie's son) for *Rolling Stone* magazine. I think it turned out pretty well. In his case it was like all the others. I just chat with people, and truly try and get to know them, almost interview them. When people begin to tell their story, it's like something from the inside comes out. As a photographer, I'm reminded of this: How do you make people forget that you have a camera in your hand? Be respectful.

I want to be a legacy photographer, meaning the images are timeless and iconic. The only way to get that is to do my best to know the subject, let them be comfortable and be themselves.

**WAYNE:** As you look back on your portfolio over the years, what are some of the most powerful moments that stick out in your mind?

**DAVID:** I recently got to do a shoot with Jerry Lee Lewis. It was for a magazine article. He actually doesn't do many interviews or photoshoots anymore. He is eighty-four now, I think, and his health has been declining. We were excited when we got the call to go to his home. His people had let us know to go ahead and get set up, be ready, and that when he comes out, it will be brief. We got there, got all set up, and were ready to go. He came and sat at the piano while we chatted. I found a way to get up over him on a ladder from behind. I was looking down at his hands on the keyboard. Here are these eighty-four-year-old hands that could tell many a story. We were all almost stopped in our tracks when he softly began playing "Somewhere Over the Rainbow." It was very surreal. I almost couldn't believe that I was in the room, much less getting to snap images. And, just like that, he was done and signaled that our time was up. He walked back out of the room. That was a huge memory.

Also, when we shot Dolly Parton, it was amazing. What you think she would be like is exactly who she is. At first, I was just getting images of her sitting in a room in front of an old window. Then I handed her a guitar. From the moment I put a guitar in her hand, she started beaming. She started playing, singing, laughing. The entire room was smiling, too. She started singing some old gospel tunes. Those were the images we kept. It was another time that I was in awe to be in the room, but I was trying to stay focused on the gig. I was also reminded of how much these artists' work is a such a huge part of them. The music really comes from within them.

**WAYNE:** So cool. With all these folks, has there ever been an artist that you were such a fan of, it distracted you from taking photos of them?

**DAVID:** Most of the time I'm cool because I'm in the zone, and there are so many things to be thinking about in terms of the work, that I don't get too distracted. But, yes, this happened with Eric Clapton. We were with him doing a shoot for an album cover, and I was just working away, staying focused. We did a few test shots with a polaroid type camera. And I remember laying the shots out on the ground, and it really hit me, I was like, "Holy cow, that's Eric Clapton! He did stuff with the Beatles!" I had to compose myself and get back to it. But it was pretty awesome.

**WAYNE:** What advice would you give to someone who might be reading this in terms of work ethic? As we are talking about this thing "meraki," which means putting your whole self into what you are working on, what comes to mind for you?

**DAVID:** Don't focus on the money, but focus on the work you are putting your hand to. For me, I want my work to remain timeless, and not dated. So, I don't get distracted by everchanging flashy trends. I would say have a strong work ethic. Be persistent, don't give up. In most cases things won't unfold like you thought they would. Luck probably has a little to do with it. I'd also say don't be afraid to critique yourself and your own work. Search out and examine the weakness in your work. As an artist, like in many areas of life, the minute you quit pushing yourself, evaluating yourself, you're done.

# ALBERT HANDELL

*"When I'm squeezing out the tubes of paint in the morning, it's like I'm walking up the steps of the metropolitan in New York where I used to live. The noise changes from the subway and the street, it starts to fade away as I'm walking up and up."*

This past year I tried something for the first time ever. I attended a multi-day oil painting workshop that was taught by a modern-day master, Albert Handell. Albert lives and paints in Santa Fe, New Mexico. Since 1961, he has had over thirty-one one-man shows and has received over seventy prizes and awards, both nationally and internationally. That means I could list them all out here, but it would take up several pages. He is eighty-three and still going strong, creating amazing pieces that are in high demand.

I normally work with acrylic paints, watercolor, and other mediums, but oil painting is its own animal. I wanted to try it out and learn from one of the best. When I rolled up on his address to see this adobe building covered with snow, I knew I wasn't in Houston anymore. There would only be three of us hanging out with Albert for the next several days. The nuggets of wisdom that I got from my time with him were more than I can share here.

The first day, the things that we talked about were pretty technical, but as time went along, he started dropping words of wisdom all over the place: "One brush stroke at a time, take it easy . . .. Each area counts. At this point, you're done worrying about the whole big picture after you mark out the spaces. Now every area counts."

At times he would make musical references while painting, which I totally connected with. "I'm just putting a note here, a note here," and "I'm just asking a question. Does the whole symphony need this note? If not, I just take it out."

I also found out pretty quickly that Albert is hilarious. Often, he would walk around our work while painting in the studio. Sometimes he would offer to show us a few things on our canvas. Albert asked to show one of the painters a few suggestions, and he said, "Of course!"

Albert said, "If there's something I'm doing to your painting you don't agree with, I'd love to know it. I don't want to hear it . . . but would love to know it . . . I always say the great thing about oils is that they're wet. But problem with the bloody medium is that they're wet . . . I'm very thankful to have done art for the majority of my life. I haven't had a job in sixty years."

When one lady was with Albert as he started to clean his brushes at the end of the day, she saw over his shoulder and asked, "What kind of soap do you use on your brushes, Albert?"

"Lava," he said. "Any soap will do, love." I think we were all thinking he was about to name some soap bar from France that all the top artists use. We were reminded that he still has to clean his brushes at the end of the day like everyone else, and he uses soap. He reminded us that fancy equipment doesn't necessarily get you the outcome you think you need.

I was sharing with Albert how we have some family in Ruidoso, New Mexico. It's beautiful up there in the mountains. On top of that, it's a quaint, small-town community. If I could only figure out a way to make a living there, I'd be set. I also mentioned growing weary of living in the Houston area metroplex that has like 7 million people. His response:

"Yep. You can either live in an area that's depressed, or that's depressing."

One of the most brilliant takeaways for me from what Albert shared was his focus on "transitioning." We do an amazingly poor job of this in our hurried world, at least I do. I rush from being on the phone, to answering my kids, to sending an email, to this, to that. He talked about transitioning from one thing to the next, it's importance, and being intentional about it. This allows you to be fully present with what you are putting your hand to. I'll always remember this moment in the studio. He started walking around his palette table, which is where you place all the colors out that you are planning to use on your painting.

"When I'm squeezing out the tubes of paint in the morning, it's like I'm walking up the steps of the metropolitan in New York where I used to live. The noise changes from the subway and the street, it starts to fade away as I'm walking up and up."

He continued walking around his table, slowly squeezing out different colors of paint.

"It's slowly preparing me for what's next. I don't like to talk while I'm doing this. Take it for what it's worth."

I stood there in silence. This man knows the importance of transitioning from the busyness of whatever is happening in the moments before, to getting his heart and mind ready to pour into his craft. This truly meant a lot to me, and I do my best to apply this to my own life today.

At the end of the few days together, he was very merciful toward my attempts at oil painting.

"Wayne, I actually love your painting. Especially since three days ago you didn't know white from black."

What a thrill to spend several days with Albert Handell. He is an inspiring artist, but more than that, he is an inspiring human. Albert has a beautiful way of bringing things from the lofty heavenlies of "awe-inspiring work," down to the reality that we, too, could make work that matters.

His heart and soul come through in every single piece . . . actually, in every single stroke of the brush.

I don't know about you, but I want that.

## SOME THINGS TO KICK AROUND

1. How did this chapter about meraki make you feel?

_____

_____

_____

_____

_____

_____

_____

2. Why do you think it is rewarding for people to put their whole self into things?

_____

_____

_____

_____

_____

_____

3. When do you feel most fully alive?

_____

_____

_____

_____

_____

_____

4. Here is how I will apply meraki to my life starting now:

_____

_____

_____

_____

_____

_____

# chapter five
# GET GOOD AT FAILING

> "Not being picked gives you resilience."
> —Unknown

Oh, man. I can talk about this one.

Failing. It's something we don't see praised on Instagram. Most of us want desperately to never fail at anything. In fact, now we've created some kind of phony world online where people try to appear as if we never have any failures. We can be tempted into faking it and acting like we don't fail. Ever.

In some ways I was surprised by just how many of the folks I interviewed brought up failure. I started seeing a trend. These folks weren't acting like they never failed. In fact, they were embracing it. It's the means by which you learn. It's the mechanism to improving. If you want to get better at something, fail, and fail often.

Failing does *not* equal failure.

This past week there was a huge milestone in my life in terms of my "dad heart." My daughter Elliott, who is now seven, came and asked me to remove something—her training wheels. Wait! No, already? I feel like I just assembled this bike only a year ago, late in the night on Christmas Eve. But, it's been a while. And she is ready. I grabbed a wrench and in moments they were gone. What was also gone was the complete stability they offered her as the rider. We started slowly, with my hand on the seat to give some support. She was peddling slowly trying to get a feel of how this was going to go. Even while this was happening, it was clear that it was one of those moments in life that you somehow know is coming, and when you're in it, it's just as intense as you thought it would be. She and I went up and down our driveway a few times, and then decided it was time to head out into the street and go a block or two. There would be moments where she would say, "Okay, you can let go," and I'd let go for a few seconds. I'm all in as a dad, and the last thing I wanted was for her to face plant! We did several short trips like this that day, and I got a great photo of her standing in front of the trash can dropping her training wheels in. Her confident face showed it all.

The next day we went again in the morning, and the durations of my "letting go" got slightly longer and longer. Until finally, that afternoon she was pretty much cruising around on her own. That's when it happened. And you know what I'm about to say.

Yep, she fell.

Hard.

It's the inevitable aspect of learning to ride a bike, isn't it? It's part of the process. I was sitting in the grass about 100 yards away watching her, and just as she fell, I sprung up. But before I could really even get over there, something awesome happened. She was back on again. She was up and peddling and heading my direction. I know it might sound a little fruity, but I saw a little teeny tiny window into her future. With a heart like that, Elliott won't be frozen in fear to try new things. What's better, she won't be quick to just toss in the towel after one failure and then give up.

A few years ago, my art professor from Texas Lutheran University, where I went to school and earned my degree in visual arts, was retiring. John Nellermoe had been there for years and years and was well loved by many, including me. He was having a gallery event showing of some of his art from over four decades. (Four decades!) It was his final showing before retiring, and I wasn't going to miss it. I drove over to Seguin, Texas, and enjoyed seeing him and several old friends, too.

As we got a few moments together to chat, he said something that struck me. "Yep, I think I'm retiring at just the right time. It's the perfect time in life for me and my wife, but also the change I see in students now is telling me it's the right time."

"What do you mean?" I asked.

"There's been a shift, I think, in the last couple years. Now it seems like students have lost their patience to fail. If they try something and they can't do it the first or second time, they just quit. They drop the class. You know already, Wayne, that pottery is basically the process of having to fail over and over again. This is how you master the process."

As soon as he said that, my mind was transported back to college when I was studying art. Stronger areas for me were drawing and painting. (And playing three-on-three sand volleyball.) My strong suits were *not* history, math, science, and basically anything else. But in order to get a BA in visual arts, a broad spectrum of classes must be taken, even art classes. Pottery. Yes, my mind flew back to me sitting at a throwing wheel, trying to hold this little ball of clay still so that I could pull it far enough to make a small cereal bowl.

Have you ever tried this? It's like crazy tough. If you move slightly too far in one direction, the spinning wheel starts to make the bowl wobble, then next thing you know, you lose it. Start over. Fail. Start over. Fail. Start over. Patience is needed, big time. During week one of the class, we had to make a small cereal bowl. In week two, we had to make a larger cereal bowl, but I will still on week one. Week three, a larger salad bowl was the assignment. Two months into this class, I'm still trying to make a cereal bowl without it looking horrible. I have this distinct memory of being in class, working on this assignment. On the wheel next to me was an exchange student from China, and she had her arm deep down into this beautiful vase that was spinning. I literally couldn't make a dog dish. I'm not kidding y'all, it was like two feet tall.

Mr. Nellermoe continued, "Nowadays many things provide instant gratification; students are on their phones all the time. If they can't figure it out instantly, they give up. It's like they have no Zen. The only way to learn and improve is to fail over and over, then repeat. That's how you get better."

There it was.

I have a truckload of stories I could share about failing. Whether it be in the music endeavors I've pursued, or the art ones, or even in my personal life. I've failed a ton. But I am not a "failure."

Even in the process of reaching out to people for this book, there were tons of micro failures. I would reach out to different folks who inspire me, and sometimes the person would respond with a "yes" or a "maybe." Sometimes I would get totally ignored and blown off (which always makes a person feel great). But I would just say to myself, "Hey, it's okay, this project wasn't for them."

One of the no's I got was so awesome, and believe it or not, inspiring. A person (whom I shall not name) of very well-known status in his or her field of work and influence sent me an incredible email. I'd sent a note saying it's my fiftieth year, yada yada, I'm interviewing lots of people, and I would love to have them involved. I asked for a ten- to fifteen-minute phone or Zoom chat. This person's response was epic. Basically, "Hey, Wayne, happy birthday. This book project sounds awesome; I don't believe I could do it justice. Thanks." It was the classiest rejection I've ever gotten. It was a no, but somehow felt encouraging.

As opposed to this response, forwarded to me from another somewhat well-known person (whom I shall also not name, but sure want to): "Thanks, but no, I'm basically retired now. And the last thing I want to do is have my brain picked, much less by a stranger."

For real.

Rejections and failures stink. But its okay! Each one is putting you one step closer to your yes. Sometimes you are just trying to get your bike up and rolling, and just when you feel the wind in your face, you hit a pothole and fall. It might even hurt for a minute. Be like Elliott and shake it off, jump back on. Be like the pottery student from China who, after many, many failures, now has her hand inside a beautiful vase. That vase may one day sit in the library of royalty, or it may sit in a closet, but the look of satisfaction on her face is something I well remember.

I hope some of the insights in this chapter encourage you and remind you that it is okay to fail. In fact, please go fail. It's the only way to get better at what you're putting your work to.

# CAM BECKMAN

> "Yeah, I've found that it's a very major thing, paying attention to how I'm thinking. If my mind gets going wrong, thinking either ahead, or behind, or negatively, I have to reign that in. If a shot doesn't go the way I wanted, I can't dwell on it. You let it go, and go onto the next one. That's it."

Cam is a pro golfer. In 1999 he joined the PGA tour and has four tour victories. At one point, Cam was number seventy-six in the entire world. Cam and I went to college together, and he was an art major as well. If you are pursuing golf as your profession, you have to major in something, right?

I have this clear memory of being in college, looking out of my apartment window, and seeing Cam out hitting golf balls into a field for hours. He was aiming for this electric pole 100 yards away. I watched him hit ball after ball, all of them landing in the exact same spot, at the foot of this pole. I remember thinking, *Why does he keep doing this over and over? He's hitting it right where he's aiming I think he's got it figured out!* Well, I had no clue about golf. But now I do, a little. I picked up the game eight years ago and got hooked. It's a tough sport. One moment you have to have power, the next finesse, the next precise accuracy, the next the softest touch. All the while trying not to look like an idiot hitting this little white ball into the woods, or worse, someone's house.

I wanted to chat with Cam and see how he was doing, and also pick his brain a little bit about this failing thing. We connected over a phone conversation.

**WAYNE:** What has been your biggest "up" moment in this journey, and your biggest "downer" moment?

**CAM:** I guess my best moment was when I won my first PGA tournament in 2001. It was beyond incredible. As far as my biggest downer, I don't think I really have one in particular. The entire game of golf is basically designed for you to fail. Failing is just part of the game. Personally, though, I did miss seeing my son being born; he came early, and I was out of state in a tournament.

**WAYNE:** Is being on the PGA Tour what you thought it would be like when you were twenty-one?

**CAM:** It's actually better than I thought it would be. When I was younger, there would be many nights I would just visualize myself out there. It felt like a massive burning call. When I finally got to that level, and was out there on the tour, it was awesome. It still is, even after all these years. There are only so many people in the world who get to do something on this level; it's an honor. I mean, playing against Tiger Woods several times during the height of his game, come on, it doesn't get much more challenging than that.

**WAYNE:** It seems like so much of the game of golf is mental. Somehow, staying relaxed and focused, but keeping your mind out of it. I know when I go play with some friends, I'm decent while warming up and just hitting to loosen up. But then out there on the course, in front of them, and it's time to make the shot, it's tough.

**CAM:** Imagine adding over 10,000 people watching, plus being on TV, and you're teeing off with Tiger.

**WAYNE:** Gulp. No thanks.

**CAM:** Golf is like life. There's continually a new obstacle to face or overcome, new challenges. Literally I learn new things every time I go play. It never ends, it's never perfect. Wait, now that I think about it, life is easier than golf. Putting, for example. It's just one of many areas of the game that is set up for you to fail. They place the hole in everchanging tough spots. I practice putting constantly. I even have a putting green in my house. I love it. All the guys you see at the higher level are literally working on it, and working out, all the time. You can't let yourself get to a point where you are not learning anymore!

**WAYNE:** Tell me more about the mental side of things.

**CAM:** Yea, I've found it's a major thing, paying attention to how I'm thinking. If my mind gets going wrong, thinking either ahead, or behind, or negatively, I have to reign that in. If a shot doesn't go the way I wanted, I can't dwell on it. You let it go, and go onto the next one. That's it. There have been times when just as I was getting my game dialed in, I would have an injury or a setback. You press on and press through.

**WAYNE**: Sounds like life just a tad. You made a change a few years ago, tell me about that.

**CAM**: Five years ago I intentionally stepped off the PGA tour and stopped playing full time. My kiddos, who were nine and twelve at the time, were growing up right in front of my eyes, and I didn't want to miss it. I knew it was time to back off when each time I would fly out to a tournament, I would get this big pit in my stomach. I wanted to be home. Now, in the last several years, I've been wearing a different hat, it's been great. Still playing golf, but not full time. Family is more important. I had to keep the right mentality then, too, that there's more to life than golf.

**WAYNE**: This is a question that I've been asking lots of people in these chats. What would fifty-year-old Cameron Beckman tell twenty-one-year-old Cameron Beckman?

**CAM**: Hmm . . . great question. I think I would say, "You have what it takes; you're not inferior." When I came down to Texas from Minnesota for school, there was this underlying pressure. I'd be playing in tournaments against guys who were from Texas A&M or UT, or these bigger schools. I had this, "I'm less than" kinda thing going on. If I could talk to twenty-one-year-old Cam right now, I'd say let that go. You have what it takes.

**WAYNE**: That's powerful, man. And I'd go back with you and tell those other guys—hey look at Cam now, y'all!

Cameron turned fifty this year (like me) and will be jumping back into golf full time again this year (unlike me). Look for him on the senior PGA tour. I can't believe I just typed that. "Senior." We are seniors, Cam (at least by golfing standards).

# TWO PINE TREES

*"If I'm honest, most of my dreams are pretty self-driven, or me oriented. But to put work and sweat and determination behind a vision that will bring joy to another, that's the gold right there, I think."*

Well, I was out here again on my family's land writing the current chapter, and I was ever so gently reminded of a great example of failure to share with you.

After we purchased this land, we dreamed and brainstormed about what to do out here. There was no cabin, no electricity, no nothing. Just rolling Texas land, cows meandering, pecan and oak trees all over the place. There is one section that is pretty heavily wooded, with a clearing that opens up into an open field. I thought, *Hey, I'll plant two pine trees out here, right as this clearing opens up.* I'll plant them twenty-five to thirty feet apart, and they will be this majestic entryway into that open field. One day when these are fully grown, it'll be my dream to sit underneath one, book in hand, and hear the sound that only a pine tree can make in the breeze. And one day, maybe we will have kids, and I'll be able to say I planted these with my bare hands. I imagine twenty years down the road, and there they are, two giant pines acting as the natural cathedral archway into the open field of glory. Yes!

The next time we came out to the land, I stopped at a garden and tree company and purchased two pine trees, each roughly ten feet tall in a twenty-gallon-sized planter. We found the perfect spot, and off I went to work. Digging, that is. Digging and digging in the Texas heat. Let me just say, I underestimated what it would take to dig not only one of these holes by hand, but two. My sweet wife would encourage me every hour or so and say, "Go, baby!" Then she would return to reading her book. About six hours later, and five gallons of sweat, the trees were in the ground. Yes! Take that, Mother Nature!

I had Kelley snap a few photos of me standing next to the trees, shovel in hand, for posterity. Remember, my plan is to show my kids, and future grandkids, how it all began. We brought several giant water jugs, and soaked them so they could get a good running start.

About two weeks later, my wife decided to come out to the land and do a few things. A few hours later, my phone rang. She said, "I kinda have some bad news, honey."

"What's wrong?" I asked. My mind was racing with what in the world could have happened. She said, "I'm sending you a couple pictures now from my phone so you can see."

Ding. Ding. The messages came in.

There it was. But what it was, I couldn't really recognize. It was a big stick just poking out of the ground.

"What am I looking at?" I asked Kelley over the phone.

"It's one of the trees you planted. I think that the cows came and basically rubbed on it so hard that they broke off all the branches. And the top. And all the bark is gone. The tree is a total goner."

"What! Wait . . . what about the other one?"

"Here's a pic of the other one. It's totally gone. And what's worse, one of the cows placed a huge cow pie where the tree had been."

Pause. Let's just pause here please and let this sink in.

Those dang cows basically sent me a message saying, "No. No, thank you. This is actually our house and we'll have something to say about what goes where out here." I could not believe that after all that work, they had destroyed them so quickly, and had left me a little poop gift on top!

Failure. I had a great plan—a great plan! Can't you just see that majestic pine tree archway in your mind? The sun beaming through in shafts of light and glory. They say, "You may enter into our open field beyond our gate." It was a Tolkien-sized plan for our land. But it was not working out. Did I give up? No, thank you.

Two months later, I was out there again, y'all. Two more new pine trees. More money! This time I picked a spot closer in to where our cabin might end up, with sandier soil. It would still be a perfect entryway into the open field behind. So, off I go, again. Digging. Digging. Six hours later, again, these two were in the ground. More watering. No photo shoot this time, too risky.

A month later, we came back out. I brought several huge containers of water so I could give my trees a drink. We pulled up, and I could see one tree. Not two. We parked and walked over to inspect. Sure enough, the cows and I were now officially in full-scale combat. One of the trees was totally annihilated. But the other one was still alive with a sliver of hope of surviving.

That's it. This was war. I drove straight to the nearest farm/ranch supply store and bought barbed wire. I'd never once in my life purchased barbed wire, so I really looked like I had no idea what I was doing. I also got ten metal stakes and headed back. I thought, *I'm going to basically fence in this tree, and there's no animal that will be able to get near it! I'm gonna get this tree to grow if it's the last thing I do.*

So, there I was. A guy from the city, trying to figure out how to make the smallest and shortest barbed-wire fence you have ever seen. I put the stakes in a circle surrounding the tree and did three rows of barbed wire. It looked super rough. Droopy is another word. What's worse, about the time I was finished, a man from the neighboring property was walking on his land. He was dressed in all camo, with a hunting bow in his hand. I'm sure he was thinking, *What is this guy doing? Why would he plant a tree out here when there's like hundreds of trees all over?* He said, "If you need any help fixing that fence, I can give you a hand."

"No thanks, I'm good." *What do you mean fix it? It's brand-new! I did that. And it's awesome.*

Not really. It was a wreck. But I thought it should at least keep the cows, and maybe the one bull, out of there.

A few months went by, and the lone tree kept growing. A few months turned into a year, and there she stood. A year turned into a few. Then came the arrival of our first little girl, then the second. It's been a huge joy to come out with them and create special "off the grid" memories together. Each time we would come out, I bring a few big water containers to give the tree some refreshment.

Fast-forward to last month. We came out together as a family with our girls. The tree is now about forty feet tall, and it's beautiful. I thought that the time of needing the old barbed-wire fence around her could finally come to an end. As the girls played and laughed outside our cabin, I took down the sad-looking fence I had put up nine years before.

There is stood. She'd made it. This dream I had back then has become somewhat of a reality.

That's when something really beautiful happened.

Elliott, who is reading like crazy these days, walked by carrying a blanket and a book. "Where are you headed?" I asked.

"I'm going to sit under the tree and read." She had the cutest smile on her face.

That's when it hit me. The dream I'd had nine years ago was to plant a tree, and that one day I'd be able to sit underneath it and read. I stood there astonished as I saw my daughter spread out her blanket, sit underneath it, and open up her book. Tears started rolling down my face. Nine years ago, I never dreamed that we would have two daughters, much less that one of them would be under that tree reading.

It's totally okay to have a dream, however big or small. Dream big! Dream often! And when it comes to fruition—celebrate. Sometimes it takes tons and tons of work for a dream to become a reality. Sometimes it takes gallons and gallons of water, barbed-wire fencing, and grit.

What really makes a dream something worth chasing is when it can have a positive impact on someone else's life. If I'm honest, most of my dreams are pretty self-driven, me oriented. But to put work and sweat and determination behind a vision that will bring joy to another, wow . . . That's the gold right there, I think.

Fail. Fail often. Repeat. Failing isn't the definer. It will happen no matter what. It just puts you one step closer to figuring things out. And maybe someone will benefit from your failing over and over. Maybe someone will lie on a soft blanket in the sunlight underneath the fruit of all your labor.

Remember I said I was currently out here at our land typing this book? Well, this morning I woke up and walked out to a glorious day, went to my truck, and realized I had left my keys in the ignition and turned to the "on" position. All night. Yep, dead battery. Out in the middle of nowhere. So you see, fail and fail often, it's a real thing. Now I'm off to go figure this out.

# BEN CHAI

*"I thought . . . It would be pretty cool to join a band, but that it would be a terrible idea."*

Ben Chai is a member of the band Streetlight Cadence. They are a folk/pop/street performing band based in Los Angeles, California. Their YouTube show *Will Play for Food* is a hit. I had fun catching up with Ben . . .

**WAYNE:** Tell me about the adventure that you have been on, Ben.

**BEN:** I guess it starts with a brief history of the band Streetlight Cadence. My brother-in-law is a founding member of the band, and we grew up together in Katy, Texas. He got a scholarship and went off to Hawaii. Other than tuition money, he was completely broke. After a few days, he had very little options other than going out and street performing. You're at your most vulnerable when street performing; some people would even argue it's one of the purest forms of making art or music. The audience is right there, you basically create your own stage, you can get shut down at any time, so yeah, its vulnerable. In 2010 he formed the band and was dating my sister at the time. (They are now married.) So, in many ways, I've been involved in some way since the beginning. But I will say . . . me, being from Katy, which is a very career-driven, over-achieving-type community, I'm a driven-type individual. When I would look at my brother-in-law doing the street performing thing, I would think, *Wow, what are you doing with your life? What happened?* Obviously not knowing that eight years later, I would be joining the band.

I graduated college, took a good and steady job. After a year and a half, I took a job with a local church, Grace Fellowship, overseeing the production and media team, where the one and only Wayne Kerr leads worship.

**WAYNE:** Nice! Yes, we loved having you work with us, man.

**BEN:** That's also where I met the love of my life, Maria. We got married. I worked there for about three years, and it was awesome. It was definitely one of those things where God taught me to listen to my gut. And also, to serve Him in ways I'd never really imagined . . . Spiritually, I was becoming more comfortable. We had our son during this season, too. Then about two and a half years into the job, my best friend was arrested for doing something really bad, and six months later he took his own life. Within a two-week period, my best friend took his own life, our son was born, and Hurricane Harvey hit Houston. Those three things combined woke me up a bit, I'd say.

**WAYNE**: Unreal that all those things were happening at the same time. I remember you feeling as if some big change was just around the corner for you guys.

**BEN**: Right after that, my brother-in-law shared that one of the guys was leaving the band. And I remember thinking, *It'd be pretty cool to join a band, but it would be a terrible idea.* Just all things considered. But something was tugging at me. I was feeling a degree of discomfort. The second I feel too comfortable doing something, maybe it's just the wiring in me, but I know it's time to shake things up.

**WAYNE**: It helps to be aware that when things become too comfortable, you can slip into being complacent. Then you end up going through the motions.

**BEN**: There's something amazing about putting your hand to something for sixty years straight; there's integrity in that. I'm just not wired in that way. To put it into perspective, I went to five universities. The second I felt like something wasn't doing it for me, I'd change. I know that would be a hard thing for some people . . . I'm just wired in such a way that is okay doing that kind of thing. I didn't do those things without counsel, a ton of conversations, and immense amounts of prayer.

**WAYNE**: So, then you felt a nudge to get plugged in to Streetlight Cadence? Tell me about that.

**BEN**: So, my brother-in-law was in town visiting, and literally was getting in the car heading to the airport to fly back to LA. I felt this nudge, and I looked him in the eye and asked what he thought about me auditioning for the new open spot. His eyes got really huge. They said, "Yes, if I was serious about it." So, after much conversation with my wife, and prayer like crazy, we did it. With a six-month-old in hand, we uprooted everything and headed to LA where there would be no stable income for us.

**WAYNE:** You crazy, man. Mic drop moment.

**BEN:** There were several things along the way that were confirming for me. One of the first big things was housing. I'm sure you know, but housing in LA is difficult. Especially if you're renting, and on top of that, we had a dog and a baby. I sent out hundreds of applications and got denied over and over. I had no proof of income obviously, but when you're in a band, you are basically freelancing. We had no residential history in LA. I had put in my two-month notice at Grace, and the clock was ticking until our moving day, and we had no place to move to.

Well, I was talking with my sister about this, and she just put out a blanket statement on Facebook saying her brother is moving to LA and looking for housing. My sister got a response from a lady who happened to be one of my best friends from Katy, Texas, who was now living in LA. They were living in one house, and their brother was living in one of the single bedroom units, and believe it or not, were about to be looking for renters for the other single bedroom unit. It was wild. They said they'd love for us to be renting from them and basically become their neighbor. Over the time there, we built a great bond with them. They became our family, really, even helped us with babysitting.

The other thing was, I had this incredible urge in my heart to learn how to play drums. I play guitar and cello and a few other things, but have always wanted to try and pick up drums. The spot I was going to fill with Streetlight Cadence was on guitar. Just after we found the apartment and had set a moving date, John, my brother-in-law in the band, called me. He said, "I know this might sound weird, but would you consider still joining us but actually becoming our drummer?" I said, "You know I don't own a drum set, I've never really played drums in my life, but if this is what God wants me to do, I'm down!" You know this was all fun and an adventure, but in the back of my mind I kept thinking, *Ben, there is literally nothing good about this situation!*

As this door was opening up, the fact that what was in my heart was now starting to match reality was a confirmation deep in my gut. Not to mention that my wife was being so supportive, too.

**WAYNE:** Tell me about the TV show you guys put together. Was this something already in the works when you moved out there? Tell me about the show and some of your adventures with that.

**BEN:** The guys had been working for a couple of years on this idea for a TV show that was more of a travel show than a music show. They'd shop it around, getting feedback. When I moved out there, I came with a bunch of video and production knowledge, as that was my job back at the church. I had some degree of experience that they didn't have in all that. Two months after I joined the band, we got greenlit to make the TV show *Will Play for Food.* It was going to play on the CBS affiliate in Hawaii. This is how I learned that relationships, more than anything else, will get you places. It's true of networking and business relationships and everything, but I think it's true of God, too. For example, all it took for us to have a network show, was for us to knock on the door of the president of CBS in Hawaii. We walked into the building with our instruments and managed to get a sit-down meeting with him. We showed him our one-minute sizzle reel. He said, "I love it, I'll give you guys Wednesday nights." The band had tried all of these schmoozing things, meeting with network people, but it really just took us being vulnerable and saying, "Look, here's what we've got." We got signed on for thirteen episodes. It became the biggest network show in Hawaii.

Basically, the show was about the band doing what they have always done, which is street perform. We would travel to a new city, usually the flight would be sponsored. But then we had to set up and play music somewhere and earn our way to food and housing. Sometimes we would be feasting because we made $300 in one hour, or it would be all four of us splitting one hamburger. That actually happened in D.C. The idea of the show was to prove that if you really work hard, it will happen, but you have to hustle. Sometimes it's not gonna be fun. If you have that spirit in you, if you have that drive, and you are willing to even delight in the suffering, it'll happen. For us, it happened in the form of an Emmy nomination. We don't even know how that happened. It was for our episode in New York City. We got shut down by the police six times over the course of one hour. Each one of the officers was actually really cool and told us they loved what we were doing, but we just couldn't do it there. Even in light of all that's going on right now with the police and tensions, I was reminded that those guys are people, too, and their job is hard. When you can have a good relationship with someone who may be about to arrest you, it goes to show that at the most fundamental level, we are much more than our occupations. We are much more than our races, our social classes; we are all people.

**WAYNE:** You guys did an episode in Tokyo, Japan, too, right? And had a little run in with the law there as well? How did you guys end up over there?

**BEN:** We were invited to perform at a week-long arts fair in Tokyo. We would sound check for an hour, then play for an hour, then be off for the rest of the day. For us, if we are visiting a location, we may as well go out and hustle. We went to shoot an episode on our off hours. It was the first episode of the show, but it was also one of the three episodes where we could have been deported. As we came to discover, there's definitely different degrees of stringency on street performing (a.k.a. busking). In Tokyo, it's totally illegal. It's not just a legal thing, but a cultural thing, like asking for money is a big no-no. So, thankfully, the police there were kind, and, also thankfully, one of our band mates is married to a Japanese woman, and he could speak somewhat fluently.

**WAYNE:** So funny. Several years ago my wife, Kelley and I got to go to Japan. I was playing some music over there, and I distinctly remember visiting Shinjuku Station. (The largest train station in the world.) There were so many cultural things that differ from the U.S.. For instance, I couldn't find a single trash can in the entire station. I also noticed how clean it was—they have a less disposable society.

**BEN:** That train station was one of the places we actually got stopped by the police as well. We couldn't play for money, but, we discovered we could play for food. So, we made a sign that said, WILL PLAY FOR FOOD and put it inside an open guitar case. We started playing and after about five minutes, a guy walked up and gave us a bag of food. That kept on happening. By the end of that busking session, we were covered in food, bottles of water, candy, everything except money, basically. It was one of those "beyond language" moments. These passersby were just helping us out; it was amazing.

**WAYNE:** Is that where you guys got the name of the show?

**BEN:** Yep, that was it. *Will Play for Food* was born. Overall, the show was a huge experience, but really hard, too. Tons of work, physically demanding, very tight deadlines, but for those thirteen weeks, it was a whirlwind. I'm a believer that if you do things right, God will provide. Making that show was the epitome of bare-bones living for us. Very stressful, too. It brought me closer to family, closer to God. It reminded me that we can do a lot to build our careers, get accolades, reach for that Emmy, reach for that Grammy. But what really matters is when, at the end of the day, we come home to our family and get a hug from them. On our resume, we'll have all that work stuff, but in our eulogy, our family and our favorite flavor of pie is what's going to be important.

**WAYNE**: Very true Ben. So, are you guys done with the show at this point?

**BEN**: We actually shopped it for two solid months. We took our instruments and went to every single TV station, streaming service, and corporation in LA. I'm talking eighty offices that we got past the security guard, talked to a receptionist, and out of all of those, maybe five let us have a meeting. None of those meetings have turned into anything yet. You're talking about getting good at failing, and how failing doesn't make you a failure. For us, it comes back to this: you have to have guts; you have to go out there and do it. The people that I know who've had success to great measure are not necessarily the most talented. They are not the most amazing at their craft or their art. But they are the people who are okay with being embarrassed. Who are ready to be rejected. A lot of those fears wore off because the band is street performers. Before I joined, the first three years of the band in LA, they literally street performed every night for six hours, seven days a week, for three years straight.

**WAYNE**: Wow.

**BEN**: That's what it took for us to get connections to Disney, the TV show, to get us gigs with Penatonix, Nick Jonas, Jennifer Hudson. All these gigs came from us working. Someone saw us playing on the street enough times, and they decided to say, "Hi."

**WAYNE**: Grit. Some people will just quit when it takes real grit to keep at it. What is crazy hearing about you guys knocking on those eighty doors and basically getting seventy-five rejections, it just means you are one step closer to the "yes" than everyone else. With that kind of work ethic and also trusting in God, who knows where it will all lead? If I'd have told you a couple years ago the list of things you guys would have already accomplished—Disney, the Emmy nomination, a top show in Hawaii, gigs with Penatonix—you probably wouldn't have believed me.

**BEN:** If you are doing what God is calling you to do, it'll be okay. And if you're supposed to suffer, you'll be okay in the suffering, too. With all of this stuff with the band, even if nothing great or huge ever happens, if God is saying to be in it, I'll keep going for it. Even if all it does is change me.

Fast-forward to just a few months ago, we had been talking about moving back to Texas just before our son would start preschool. We really wanted our families around for this phase in his life. With the success of the TV show, and the band in general, it was working out for us to be able to fly to do events. The band was doing better than ever, we had gotten signed with an agent, we had so much lined up: tours, events. If any year were to be the year, 2020 was going to be the breakthrough year for the band. And then Covid-19 happened. With the pandemic, it all just disappeared.

I told the band that the absolute worst thing that could happen during this pandemic would be if we broke up. So, I'm going to move to Katy, Texas. We now have to figure out how to live as a band while not all living within driving distance. How do we work together in this modern time and in this situation? How do we keep a good work ethic in all this? As far as the career side of things, it's all a leap of faith. I actually didn't know if the guys would still like me as a person if I up and left to come back and be settled here. That's the reality we are living right now. So, I can't say how this will all play out. But I can already tell, something that's happening is that we as a band we are more and more concerned with each other's lives. Now when we call one another, it's more real, more honest. One of the guys in the band, his wife is a nurse and she's in the middle of taking care of patients in LA. We check in on each other first before we do our business, which is way different for me. I feel like if there were ever a time to slow down and actually have deep spiritual discussions, this is the time. For better or for worse, we aren't busy anymore. We still get to create. But great things are happening with us.

**WAYNE:** Okay, last question. What would thirty-one-year-old Ben tell twenty-year-old Ben?

**BEN:** What comes to my mind has nothing to do with all we've been talking about. I don't think I told you, but one of my best friends growing up passed away this past week after battling an illness. He was my age. I'm still processing it, honestly. He had gotten married just a few years ago right after his diagnosis, and his son is due in a month.

**WAYNE:** Man, I'm so sorry.

**BEN:** Twenty-year-old Ben would have never imagined any of that happening. I'm trying to put into words what I would say . . . This friend of mine, he took a job in New York, and he would fly back once a year, usually during the holidays, and we would all connect. I remember thinking when I was twenty years old, that if we all live to be seventy or something, I might only get to see him fifty more times. If it's once a year like this. I never imagined that it would be only ten more times. You know what? I would tell my twenty-year-old self it's okay to bug people.

By that I mean it's okay to call everyone I know once a week. Whenever a friend calls me it's like the best thing in the world. I hope for it and yearn for it. Yeah, I'd say it's okay to call and check in with people, it's okay to meet up at Whataburger, it's okay to go beyond a text, and it's okay to check in more than once a year. Yep, that's what I'd tell myself.

**WAYNE:** That's beautiful, man. You have always been about real relationships. When we worked together at Grace, there was a reason why the media department you were managing thrived. It wasn't because you talked about camera angles and white balance and lighting and all that; it was about relationships. People felt loved. People felt like, *Ben gets me. Ben cares about me.*

## SOME THINGS TO KICK AROUND

1. Do you think it's okay to fail? What are some times in your life you have failed at something?

2. Does failing mean that you're a failure?

3. Here is how I will apply "Get Good at Failing" to my life starting now:

*chapter six*

# SIGNIFICANCE VERSUS SUCCESS

"They may forget what you said—but they will never forget how you made them feel."[15]

—Carl W. Buehner

During the season in my life that I was putting out albums every two years or so, it was a busy and beautiful time. Over that sixteen-year period of doing music full time, I experienced a ton. One weekend my band guys and I would be in front of 4,000 screaming teenagers. The next week I'd be playing in front of twenty-seven people, some not listening and some walking out. I never knew what to expect.

In 2012, we put out an album called *Love Stands Out*. It was one of my favorite projects that I've made to date. It was also my first time to take a swing at putting a song of mine on the radio. As an independent artist, there was no record label or company promoting us. So, I hired a radio promoter for a few months to give it a try.

The song "The Mirror" was the tune the radio promoter suggested for us to try. Over the coming couple weeks, we would get reports back from him. We would even get a spreadsheet of all the stations, and it would indicate them saying "no," "yes," or "not right now." It was brutal to have station managers basically say no to a song that you had poured your life into, but that's the music business, right? I remember when the promoter would text me and say things like, "Lake Monticello added the song." And I'd be like, "Great! Where is Lake Monticello?" (I'm just making up the name here for effect, but you get my point.) Basically, very, very small towns and small stations were adding my song to their playlist.

Each time, I would jump up and down and celebrate the small victory. Who knows who will hear my song in those places? It was a fun time. Well, I remember distinctly one day Raz (bass), Nolan (guitar), and myself were out playing golf. This was not a frequent occurrence, but it was fun when we could get together. My phone buzzed with a text, and it said, "Tampa has added." Now, Tampa I had heard of! Five minutes later, he texted again, "Chicago has added." I literally dropped my club and started running around in circles screaming for joy on the golf course.

Now, hear me. "The Mirror" never became a huge hit around the world. But it was number twenty-three in Christian radio for a bit.

The song has a fun, lighthearted piano pop feel to it. But, more importantly, the message is strong. It talks about how much pressure the world puts on us to appear to have it together on the outside. Now more than ever, in this social media world, an entire generation of young people is seeing the need to compete with everyone else. There's an underlying pressure to look good, show how successful you are, and so on. This song talked about how, as referenced in the Bible, humans look at the outside, while God looks at the heart.

During those weeks and months that the song was on the radio, my favorite moment was this. I received an email from a young lady somewhere in Minnesota. She said she was driving down the road, changed the radio station, and my song "The Mirror" came on. She said once it started, she was so gripped by the message that she had to pull her car over and just park. She went on to share that it brought her to tears, and truly encouraged her that day. She was reminded of God's love for her heart, not just what she was wearing, or looked like, or least of all what others had to say. She said later that day, she spent time contacting the radio station so she could find out who the song was by, then found my website and wanted to email me to say thanks.

I remember that night reading that email, and it brought tears to my eyes. It was a significance versus success moment for me. Looking back now, all the way to 2012, no one remembers or cares that a song of mine was number twenty-three on the charts for a while. But that very special young lady remembers a day when a song so moved her heart, that she had to pull over and truly listen.

That moment for me made all of the months of work on the album completely worth it. Weeks and weeks of writing, pre-production rehearsals, studio time, mixing decisions, mastering, and cover decisions—all of that was worth it to receive that single email.

# FERNANDO ORTEGA

> "I remember there was one album I released that had tunes about a
> dragonfly, a coyote . . . I loved that record. It was a dismal failure."

Today I'm sitting at a table inside of the iconic Mary & Tito's restaurant in sunny Albuquerque, New Mexico. This little café has been here since 1963. Today I'm meeting up with Fernando Ortega to grab lunch and chat. I've been super pumped for this time for weeks. Fernando is an incredible singer-songwriter who has had a great impact on me, not only in terms of music, but on my heart as well. My wife and I had our first dance as a married couple at our wedding reception to his song "Lonely Road." His music is deep waters. Much of his work is pretty introspective, mellow, and very worshipful, while some is more akin to folk music. As a fellow piano guy, I'll say I am pretty picky about piano players and the arrangements they bring. Fernando has a special gift. If you listen through one of his albums, you're not just gonna hear four chords over and over; this guy is a skilled writer. He has written tunes about his grandfather, his daughter, a homeless woman, and God's creation. Many of the songs that have deeply connected with his audience are often his arrangements of hymns and the liturgy. Some of his most well-known pieces are "Jesus King of Angels," "Sing to Jesus," and "Our Great God." And he is not afraid to write songs of doubt, distress, and longing. At the same time, from what I've seen from some of his concert events, he also has a lighthearted personality and is fairly hilarious—which I appreciate.

Fernando is an eighth generation Ortega from the small town of Chimayo, New Mexico, which is near the Rio Grande. He comes from a long line of artisans and craftspeople. His great-grandmother was an award-winning weaver. So, yeah, he has creativity in his veins. I dare you to listen to his song "Mildred Madalyn Johnson" and not start crying.

I'm excited to be sitting in this little restaurant waiting to connect with him. His manager in Nashville texted me and said he was running a few minutes late but was on his way. I'll admit the next few minutes were pretty hilarious. I positioned my chair, scooted back, scooted in, changed chairs, ate some chips, moved the chips so Fernando could easily reach them once he arrived, repositioned my chair—. Then I thought, *Get a grip, man.* What can I say, I'm a fan.

Within two minutes of being together, I realized two things: 1) He's a real person (not unlike everyone else I've connected with during this process) and 2) I really, really like this guy.

We had an amazing lunch and just got to know each other and our families. The interview below is partially from our time there and partially from a more recent Zoom interview. (Because, if I'm honest, I spent most of the lunch that day just enjoying hanging out. I'm not the master of the interview either.) My times with him have been transparent and honest.

**WAYNE:** Let's talk about significance versus success.

**FERNANDO:** I was twenty-nine when I was offered a record deal for the first time. I was in San Francisco singing for a conference and was approached by a label owner. I jumped at the chance. To be honest, I don't know if I was thinking about wealth or anything like that, but the fame and acknowledgment part sure sounded good. At the end of the day with that experience, it ended up being a horrible thing. I basically got robbed blind. I got one royalty check from that record, and it bounced.

**WAYNE:** Wow, welcome to the music industry—yikes. It seems like a constant tension exists between significance and success. A person could be driven to be creating a work that might certainly be successful in some way, fitting in with whatever trends are hot at the moment. A person could also be driven to be creating a work that, regardless of the outcome, has their full heart, sweat, tears, and handprint on it.

**FERNANDO:** There was an amazing lady, Flannery O'Connor, a very profound writer and theologian who died at the age of thirty-nine. She was well-known for her short stories. People would come up to her and ask how to be successful at writing, or ask if the university was stifling its young writers. She said, "My opinion is that they don't stifle enough of them. There's many a best seller that could have been prevented by a good teacher." Meaning, the author jumped into it with the goal of being a "success," but they turned out this crappy book that ended up being famous. She's saying when you pursue the gift God has given you, you can pursue fame, or you can pursue good writing, but they are not the same path. Sometimes, sometimes you might be blessed by having success by pursuing good writing, being true to yourself whether it be writing a book, singing a song, or whatever. If both things happen, great. But if the fame doesn't happen, and you have something you can be proud of, then that's the goal. When I think about the songs that I have written that have stuck over the past twenty-five years, they are ones that we worked tirelessly on until they shimmered. They haven't brought tons of riches, but I can be proud of them.

**WAYNE:** You are a craftsman, that's for sure, and it comes through in your work. I also appreciate your sense of humor. Tell me again the story of when your daughter was born.

**FERNANDO:** Oh, it was incredible. When our daughter was born, I remember being in the NICU unit, and it had been some time before they let me be with her. Finally, there I was, in this room with all these little babies, and standing in front of my very own child. It was just overwhelming. I looked at her face and thought, wow, she looks like my mom. I was crying all over the place and holding her little sweet toe. I started praying, praying for this little girl. I prayed that she would walk closely with God, that she would be a world-changer. It was one of the most poignant moments in my life. Next thing I knew, I felt a hand on my back, and I turned around. The nurse was standing there, and she gently said, "I'm sorry, Mr. Ortega, that's not your daughter. She is right over here."

**WAYNE:** Unreal!

**FERNANDO:** Yeah, and I was like, that first baby was actually Asian, but she still looked like my mom, I thought. Then I scooted over one spot and met my actual little girl.

**WAYNE:** Any funny recording studio stories come to mind?

**FERNANDO:** One time I was doing a guest vocal on someone's record, and the artist and his wife were in the control room, along with their producer. I was in this little vocal booth. I said, "It's so hot in here, even with my pants off,

I'm sweating." It didn't really go over very funny with anyone. I thought it was hilarious, but oh, well.

**WAYNE:** That's awesome! No response from the control room? Hilarious. Let me pick your brain on the subject of creativity. As a person of faith, the art or music that I make, I want it to be God-glorifying; I want to bring my very best work. But the tension between, *Is this Christian Art or Christian Music?* I've been wrangling with this for the past couple years. For example, exploring ideas subject-wise and musically, should it only fit within the boundaries of what works within, and for the church?

**FERNANDO:** I have songs about my grandfather, my family, life, that don't mention God per se. I remember there was one album I released that had tunes about a dragonfly, a coyote . . . I loved that record. It was a dismal failure. Mainly because they didn't know how to market it, I guess. Christian radio didn't know what to do with a song about a coyote. It was a downer for me. But I was being true to myself as a songwriter. I realized that even in these works where I'm writing about my daughter, or my family, these songs are reflective of how I feel as a Christian about these people in my life. I also realized there is music made directly for the church, which is "sacred music," and then other music obviously outside of that. I want all of it to come from a sincere heart, though. All of the years of me doing this, creating music in and through the church, there is a weird tension that exists. On the one hand, it is a pure and holy Gospel. On the other hand, it is still a business, and often those things don't go together very well.

And you know, now I look back on my life and career, and I've had several great opportunities. I've been distributed by Word and Sony, gone all over the world. But the real rewarding things have been something different than all that. Many of the songs I have written that have actually stuck with people, are often ones sung at funerals. That aspect has been rewarding to me. I don't have fancy cars or a huge house or anything, but it is okay, God has taken care of me. It's the biggest blessing knowing that some of these songs have meant so much to certain people.

Fernando and I recently connected for a Zoom chat. It was only two weeks after the loss of his mother.

**WAYNE:** I'm so sorry about your loss. It sounds like you and your mom were really close.

**FERNANDO:** We are all so close. My mom lived three miles from me. Our family is all very tight, and this has been tough.

**WAYNE:** It's been about seven years since my dad's passing. And even though he had been sick and dealing with cancer for three years, you're not prepared for when they are not here; it felt like my compass had been broken. It's such a hard thing, no matter how old you are, when it's your mom or your dad.

**FERNANDO:** I was just telling my brother yesterday, I remember being ten, and my mom had to go into the hospital for heart problems. I prayed, *God, if You'll at least wait until I'm fifteen, because maybe then I'll be able to handle it if my parents died.* Then I moved it back to twenty. Then on and on through the years. Now I'm sixty-three, and I thought I might be ready. But, yeah, it's tough. Yesterday I went up into the mountains at like 4:30 p.m., and I just stayed there until the sun went down. I just sat there watching the birds.

**WAYNE:** I saw recently that you are into bird-watching.

**FERNANDO:** Yeah, it's a funny story. One day, American Express called me and said I had like 2 million points on my card, and if I didn't use them they were going to expire. I told my manager that I maybe wanted to buy a really good camera with the points. He said I was crazy, and that my cell phone takes way better picture, not to mention I won't want to carry it around. I went ahead and bought a pretty good camera and lens, and started going out and taking pictures of birds out near our property. I'm a guy who kind of has a lot of stresses, and honestly, I don't handle stress too well. But the minute I started going out into the woods and listening for birds, it really got me. For me, it's kind of like fly fishing. When you're fly fishing, you toss it out onto the water, and watch it floating. You are so focused and concentrating to see if a fish is gonna jump on that thing. Pretty soon, you're lost in that moment, and all your stresses go away, you know? I've found the same with bird-watching. Now I've become this guy who goes out into the woods and sits on a log, listening for the tiniest little sound."

Yesterday I was really feeling sad about my mom passing away. There's kind of a low-grade anxiety to that thing. A kind of depression. I went up into the mountains and found this area by a little natural spring. There were so many sounds going on simultaneously. I literally sat on my behind for three hours just watching and listening. When I left, I can say that the sadness had lifted a little bit. All of this bird-watching stuff has taught me a lot about the imagination of God. The diversity of creation really is insane. There are certain types of birds that only forage on the ground, certain types that will only be high in the trees. In so many ways, all of this inspires someone who is a songwriter, or an artist, or a lyricist, or a singer. It reminds me, imagination can be so big, so creative, and so varied. It inspires my artistic works. Sometimes it inspires me to just come home and write a song. But then *The Simpsons* may be on TV, and I get sidetracked.

**WAYNE:** The struggle to not get sidetracked is real. I can relate on getting out into nature. For me, miles and miles of concrete can't really sooth the soul. Jesus often took off and went to be alone in the woods and mountains. I think He loved being with the animals, too.

**FERNANDO:** There's the folklore tale, in the song called "The Carol of the Birds," when all the different kinds of birds came to worship Christ. Plus, how He was born among the barn animals, too, it was the lowliest kind of scene. All throughout scripture, Jesus makes illustrations about the birds of the air, or the lilies of the field, definitely there is room in our theology for the beauty of nature.

**WAYNE:** Our family has a little cabin in Ruidoso, New Mexico that has been in my wife's family for years and years. I just love going up there anytime I can. There is this one little grouping of aspen trees that is barely making it. Each time we go, I just stand there and water them in the morning and at night, and it's so incredibly relaxing. It's good for my soul, too, to be doing my best to tend to something God has allowed me to take care of for a bit. I think, *Look at these leaves, and how when the wind blows, they do this amazing thing, and the sound is brilliant.*

**FERNANDO:** Deep water, those things. I had a friend move here, and he had some aspens and would go out there and just sprinkle the leaves a little bit . . . they all died.

**WAYNE:** Okay, one last question. What would sixty-three-year-old Fernando tell twenty-year-old Fernando, if you could tell him anything?

**FERNANDO:** Twenty-year-old Fernando was extremely full of himself. Twenty-year-old Fernando was extremely confident—confident in the wrong things. I think I would tell myself to really apply myself more to what I was good at, and to turn off the charm button. I should have applied myself to learning, to taking in scriptures better, learning more about church history, honing a theology of beauty, a theology of worship. I should have been practicing my butt off on the piano and reading great literature. Because when you are a writer, reading people who are infinitely better than you is the only way to get better.

**WAYNE:** Thank you for being real, honest, and transparent. Not only here today, but in your songs over the years. For the record, you're an awe-inspiring piano player.

# NELSON BLALOCK

*"Could I see your drawings in your art pad? Your daddy says you like to draw, I'd love to see what you're up to!"*

When I was about nine years old, a man did something that altered the course of my life. He probably didn't even know it.

Every summer as a kiddo growing up in Houston, Texas, our family would take at least one family vacation to go camping. I use the word "camping" loosely. We didn't hike any 14K peaks or go off-grid for weeks at a time with only a backpack and a pocket knife. Our idea of camping was to grab our tiny travel trailer, a tent for me and my sis, and head to the Hill Country of Texas. From Houston, it's only three and a half hours to a totally different world.

Hills. Low humidity. Fireflies. Awesomeness.

Most summers would find us in Fredericksburg, Texas. A (then) small, vibey German town rich in history. The peaches in summer are ridiculously sweet and juicy if you get a chance to visit. There is a certain campground where we would usually return each year. My dad befriended one of the men who worked part time for the park at the check-in security office. His name was Nelson Blalock.

I'll never forget the day my dad shared with me what Nelson did with the other half of his time. He was a cartoonist and illustrator for the small-town newspaper. Wait, what? We all knew very well the local cartoon strip that had a certain main character, who was a local German guy named "Fritz." I loved that guy. The character had a huge mustache, lederhosen (which is like a traditional Bavarian outfit), and a hat with a feather in it. And I loved, *loved* to draw. My art pad was like an extension of my body at this time. I went through pads and pads of art paper as a kid. I remember when I found out that the guy who was sitting in that little park entrance office was the same guy drawing these cartoons, I flipped out. I was so excited to get to meet him and talk with him in person.

My dad and I went up to the office the next day. I remember walking in and meeting him. He was burly and strong, and his warm smile could melt any heart. We talked for a minute about his cartoons, and how I loved them. Evidently my dad had shared with him that I loved to draw. He asked me a question that was so profound and huge in my life. He asked me something so giant to me, even though it may have been a small thing to him.

Do you want to know what it was?

Are you ready?

He asked, "Could I see the drawings in your art pad? Your daddy says you like to draw. I'd love to see what you're up to."

At this age, it was basically like Walt Disney opening the gates of Disneyland and asking me if I'd like to show him my portfolio.

I handed him my art pad. He smiled from ear to ear as he flipped through the pages, really truly looking at my drawings. "These are really great. Keep it up! Keep drawing!"

Those words of encouragement meant so much. More than he knew. It was like he handed me the keys to the universe. At a time when it seemed that maybe no one else in the world gave a rip that I was sitting around drawing and doodling, this kind man spoke words of life into me. Straight into my soul. He was an artist, saying that I can do it, that I should do it, and I should keep it up!

It changed everything.

Nelson had a grasp on something significant, I believe. He lived a life of significance over success.

My hunch is that I wasn't the only kid who came through there that he encouraged. Who knows the lives he has impacted. I do know that his encouraging words were like a fan to my very tiny ember of a flame of creativity. That tiny ember grew into a small flame.

At thirteen or so, I talked my parents into letting me rent a booth space at a comic book convention that was coming to town. I just knew I could sell my drawings of superheroes! They kinda thought I was crazy but supported the endeavor. It cost $75 to rent a space for the three-day event. My mom helped talk my dad into letting me borrow the money. (I had nada.) My pitch to them was, "Look guys, if I can just make $25 each day over the three days, I'll be able to pay you back in full." My parents rock, and they believed in me and lent me the money. At the end of the first day, I had sold $180 worth of drawings. My dad was so thrilled that on that very day, he rented a room in that same hotel for all of us to stay in that night to celebrate.

Nelson has been passed now for many years. My mom actually stayed in touch with his wife for years and years. I have in my office a drawing that he made and gave to me as a gift. It was an illustration of his "Fritz" character sitting in front of a canvas doing his own self portrait. Almost like an ode to some very famous Norman Rockwell works. I treasure this drawing.

Nelson would have no way of knowing that I would go on to graduate from college with a degree in visual arts—the first in my family to even go to a university.

Nelson wouldn't have known that I would have a drawing on display at the United Nations at nineteen years old.

Nelson wouldn't have known that the encouraging words of "You can do it" would help me write, record, and perform music around the country and the world. More importantly, that those songs and messages would hopefully encourage and inspire thousands in the next generation.

Nah. Nelson wouldn't have had any idea. He took ten minutes out of his day to look at some drawings that a kid did, and he spoke words of life and encouragement. He helped water a tiny seed that was already there.

I pray to be like Nelson. I pray to not be so laser focused and hell-bent on being "successful" (whatever that means) that I miss out on an opportunity to impact someone's life. A little kindness goes a long way.

Let your life be like Nelson's. Create. Enjoy. Do great and life-giving work. But more importantly, share your life and maybe even ten minutes with someone. Who knows where they will end up. Maybe, just maybe, one of the keys to "pursuing what makes you come alive" is investing in others along the way. Maybe just like a gardener who waters a seed to see it grow, you might water someone's seed of a dream. Both you and the gardener will get some joy and satisfaction from that, I'd bet.

# NOAH ELIAS

> "I'm going to go leverage the unique abilities that God gave me. What's that? That's some art, that's some speaking, that's some filming, writing, mentoring. That's a potpourri of stuff. But I'm going to focus on what gives me life, what makes me come alive, puts a smile on his face, and I'll populate Heaven while doing it."

Noah Elias is an artist, entrepreneur, author, and mentor. He and his wife, Chantel, helped create Acres of Love, a nonprofit committed to rescuing and caring for children with special needs who have been orphaned in South Africa.

I recently had read two of his books, *Fearhunters*, and *31 Disciplines of Highly Successful Creatives*. Both blew me away. It was a complete joy and honor to spend an hour with him during our Zoom meeting. If you want to talk about significance versus success, this is a voice in the world you should get to know.

**WAYNE**: Noah, tell me how your art journey started out. From what I understand, you started when you were a kid.

**NOAH**: My parents split when I was nine. When I was about to turn thirteen, I figured out I was on my own. I started a business when I was sixteen, going door-to-door on my bike. I had clients while I was in high school. When I was in my twenties, it was all about working, how do I make money. I was painting cars for *The Fast and the Furious*, I was doing kids' rooms' ceilings, I was doing tattoos, stuff for Nordstrom. Anywhere and everywhere I could get work. I was putting out flyers about my art. There was no such thing as social media. It was all word of mouth.

**WAYNE**: You are open about your faith, and I appreciate that, man. Tell me how you've felt or seen God moving in your heart and in your work.

**NOAH**: I had a crisis at twenty-eight. I'd been given the ability to paint and create whatever I wanted to, but how was I going to leverage that in my lifetime? I could paint this and that, but I felt like the Lord said, "Paint something for everybody." I wanted to reach as many people as possible. So, that year, I painted what was in my journal. All the hurts, the bad, the joys, the suffering, all of it. I took pages from my journal and used those to create honest pieces from my story. From that the Angel series came. A guy walked into my studio and said, "I want all of these original pieces for my home." It was a $48,000 purchase, and I thought, *This is insane.* That was obviously encouraging and exciting. It was a tell into what was possible.

After that I realized I had to be authentic and make art that has meaning and story to it. Where people can see themselves in it, which was a really important part. That's what I've been doing ever since. Then Disney started seeing my work, and things started to grow from there. They became one of my biggest customers, which was a blessing, too, because I was able to reach more people, share my testimony.

**WAYNE:** You talk often about significance versus success. How did that come about in your life?

**NOAH:** My art business began to be successful, but I wanted to continue to find ways to have significance, not just success. So, I started a boutique business to help entrepreneurs start, launch, and build their brand. Not for just a life of income, but also of impact. We created Noah University, an online course for helping people out in these areas.

**WAYNE:** How do you balance goals, work, and dreams—all good stuff—with family?

**NOAH:** This year I wrote a book called, *31 Disciplines of Highly Successful Creatives.* I call it fitting your work around your life, not your life around your work. Date nights with my spouse, best days with my kids. Most people, when you have 168 hours in your week, you can either spend them, waste them, or invest them. How we can create each day can be an absolute *amazing* investment. When I make my priorities align with God's priorities, things for me have just seemed to fit better.

Most believers have access to a Kingdom economy, but they continue to operate in a Babylonian economy. If you go to Matthew 6:33, "But seek first his Kingdom, and his righteousness, and all these things will be given to you as well," (NIV) it's basically God saying, if you align your priorities with my priorities, I'll take care of the back end. That's all the business stuff. When it comes to sales and development and what's successful and what isn't successful, man, I just have to say. I'm operating in a Kingdom economy, not a Babylonian economy.

**WAYNE:** Incredible. What's been a "wow" high moment, and a super low moment?

**NOAH:** It took me thirty years to become an overnight success. This isn't like, "It just happened." There've been twelve failures for every win. Learning to be a professional failure and embracing that. If you're not failing, you're not growing. It's absolutely essential for your growth. You have to embrace that, and lean into it, and be completely cool with that.

Learn. Refine. Make it better. Launch again.

It's a really hard question, because when you live that way, there really isn't a low. I mean, I've had death threats, I've had frivolous lawsuits, all kind of crazy stuff. But, I mean for leadership, that's the price of admission. A lot of leaders think, *If I have success, I won't have any more issues.* You don't learn a lot from people and their successes. You learn a lot from how people handle their failure and pressures.

As for "wow" moments, I guess some people would say, "Oh, Disney. You've reached the pinnacle." But the real wow and exciting moments have been when we helped underwrite the first Acres of Love home in Cape Town. We saw four special-needs kids come into that house. That's like seeing your kids being born! To realize that all of this work, all the hardship, is worth it when you see that moment happen.

**WAYNE:** This is all so contrary to how everyone and everything out there defines "success." It's obvious that you have a heart for sharing and mentoring creatives and entrepreneurs out there.

**NOAH:** I do. And honestly, most creatives don't have a mentor.

**WAYNE:** It's clear that your relationship with God truly drives your day-to-day, not only the big-picture things you guys are achieving, but the small decisions, too. What advice would you share for anyone reading this right now?

**NOAH:** Wake up every single day and make yourself a living sacrifice. I mean, you can take my wife, you can take my kids, you can take every bit of possession I have. You can take all the money in my bank account. I'll move wherever you want. I'll do whatever you want me to do. I am yours. When you live in that space every single morning, and remind yourself of that in the middle of the day, and in the evening, you won't be walking around disappointed. You won't really have a bad day anymore. Because you won't be trying every day to meet these false expectations you set for yourself.

For me, the word I had to surrender years ago was "agenda." But then everybody asks, "Yeah, but then what do you wake up and do?"

I wake up and do whatever is going to partner with my Father, with what's right in front of me now, which is Acres of Love work. And I'm going to go leverage the unique abilities that God gave me. What's that? That's some art, that's some speaking, that's some filming, writing, mentoring. That's a potpourri of stuff. But I'm going to focus on what gives me life, what makes me come alive, puts a smile on His face, and help populate Heaven while doing it. If more of us did that, we wouldn't be so bummed all the time, so frustrated all the time. Everybody's walking around with a problem they're trying to solve. It is like asking, How do I crack this code? People are asking the big questions, *What do I do with my time and my money, and why am I here?*

Sacrifice is the key. When we first believe Him, then it's a matter of trust. But only until you trust will you actually surrender. Most people think that's when it ends, but when it truly ends is when you become a sacrifice. That's when you're undone.

Creatives and entrepreneurs, you can take so much pressure off your life when you surrender your life. I'm talking about surrendering your will, laying yourself down as a sacrifice. Be able to say, "Whatever you want to do with me." For some people, that might not sink in during their lifetime. Others might come late to the game. For me, I'm a late learner. For some reason, God must have wanted me to know this at this specific time, and now I just want to tell the world about it.

**WAYNE:** Here's something I've been asking most folks I've been connecting with on this journey. What would forty-eight-year-old Noah tell twenty-one-year-old Noah?

Long pause . . .

**NOAH:** You have what it takes.

Make sure everything that you invest your time, talent, and money into will be waiting for you in eternity.

Can everything you invest in have eternal value?

Keep it simple.

Underwrite memories with your wife and kids.

Buy your building—don't rent it.

Invest in relationships.

## CRAIG AND MARY JUTILA

"I just saw this grace in him. Whereas, before he would have just fired them! But he was looking at other things going on in their lives currently, or in their past, looking at all of it. I can remember at one point looking at him and going, 'Oh, my gosh, my husband is so much more like Jesus than I am.'"

Craig was truly one of a kind. We lost him way too soon. My friend sadly passed away last December while on the ski slopes with his family. He was with those he loved beyond description, doing something he loved. But I know if he were here right now, he would probably say, "Not the most lighthearted and joyful way to start a story, Wayne."

Craig Jutila was hilarious, gifted, an incredible communicator and author, an insanely great guy, and on top of that, he was a truly loving husband and dad. I met Craig several years ago while doing music at a Vacation Bible School week in Dallas, Texas. He was the speaker for the week. Yes, he and I were communicating to hundreds and hundreds of kids! So fun. Insane, but fun.

For thirteen years, Craig was the children's pastor at Saddleback Church in California. He served there as the church went from a startup all the way through the massive growth of *The Purpose Driven Life*. The book had spread all over the world, and Craig was holding on with all his might to grow and maintain an exploding ministry with thousands of kids. I remember him telling the story of how he just felt he could keep adding, and adding, and adding to his plate. His heart was driven to do more and more at work and in his ministry, but all this led to a total burnout. He saw his family being sacrificed in all of it.

He once described how our lives are sort of like an extension cord power strip. You know the ones I mean? They have one plug at one end so you can plug into the wall, and then it's a strip of maybe six plugs, so you can piggy back and plug other stuff in. He said that this was him. (I could relate.) He said, "Hey, I'm good to go; I have these six or seven things I want to do, and I'm getting maxed out here. But look, I'm kinda smart, so what I'll do is just plug *another* power strip into this one!"

Craig went on to share how he maxed out the second power strip, then added a third. He said, "And you know what, people praised me for how awesome I was. People marveled at how much I could get done, how much I could juggle. And unfortunately, all of this fed my desire and need to be affirmed and recognized for what I was doing. So, it just got worse and worse."

I remember being at a conference where Craig was sharing this story and actually using it as a visual on stage. Seeing a power strip connected to another power strip, connected to more, chained to another one. It was a powerful image. I could see myself in that trap.

What about you? It's so easy for some of us to fall into this. The most powerful moment for me was at the end of this visual presentation. He said, "Here I was walking through life, and this was me. Do you want to know what's at the very end of this chain of stuff? Do you want to know what was at the tail end of all the stuff I had going on? My family. They were getting the last scraps, the leftovers. It wasn't healthy, it wasn't good, it wasn't God's plan for us."

Craig went on to share that he had such blinders on. His ministry was so huge, and he had so many irons in the fire, it all was spinning out of control. He once told me the following story: "I was burning the candle at both ends, and I had no idea that it wasn't normal, much less healthy. I was at a large national ministry conference, and I remember being one of the headline speakers. There were thousands and thousands of ministry leaders there. I spoke one session, afterward went to the bathroom, threw up some blood, and went to speak another session. It's crazy! What was I thinking? Tons of those leaders in that place wanted to be me, because hey, I'm at Saddleback, I have a giant thing going on. Little did they know how out of control I was. I finally ended up at the doctor's office, and I remember my doc saying, "You know, Craig, this isn't good."

After leaving Saddleback, he and his wife, Mary, wrote the book, *From Hectic to Healthy*, and this tool has gone on to positively impact thousands of lives. I reached out to Mary to have a Zoom chat about Craig's ministry, their lives together, and the journey she is on now. She was so very gracious to spend a little time sharing her heart.

**WAYNE:** Mary, thank you so much for taking some time to chat. Craig was an amazing guy, and he sure inspired me and so many. One of my last text message threads with him before he passed away was about this book, and he was so kind and supportive. He said to sign him up for one of the first copies. He had no idea at that time that he was on my list of people to talk to. Let's talk about the huge calling that he had on his life.

**MARY:** One of the things that was driving Craig so much was that he wanted to change the face of children's ministries at churches. That being a "children's minister" is not a stepping stone to being a "youth pastor," so that then you could climb up the food chain, if you will, to be a "college pastor," then a "senior pastor" at a church. He really believed strongly that if you felt called to children, you needed to be all in! He wanted to change things from just entertaining the kids to much more than that. He wanted to build leadership skills into the leaders. He never called the volunteers "volunteers," he called them "leaders," then equipped them. He modeled that so well.

**WAYNE:** You could easily tell that Craig's heart was to empower kids to know Jesus. He wasn't afraid to raise the bar with children and allow them to be stretched and truly learn and lead, too.

**MARY:** He started an amazing deal called "Ten for Ten." The idea was to take ten sixth graders for ten weeks and teach them all they should know before entering middle school years. It had a really high calling to be part of this small group, and take it seriously. At the end of the ten weeks, eight still were plunged in. And those eight kids said, "We love this. Can we keep going?" They didn't want to stop! The joke between us was that it became "Eight for twenty." At the end of that, we took them on a mission trip. We still have a connection with those kids today.

**WAYNE:** I know it's so hard to try and balance what you love and are called to do, with what is even more important, which is family and taking care of yourself. I can't even begin to imagine how tough it was to say no to things that were coming across his plate.

**MARY:** He was writing curriculum, leading leaders, overseeing literally the largest children's ministry in the country, speaking, and writing a book. His heart was to really equip those leaders. Then next thing you know, *The Purpose Driven Life* came out, and the children's conference along with it. You can't have a conference without materials. He was working on ways to equip those leaders, too. There were so many parts. Even with all the good things happening, it was a super hard time. Unfortunately, all of it added stress to Craig's life.

**WAYNE:** This is some of what I'm wanting to share in this chapter. Unfortunately, it seems like this natural course of things, that we build and build, we add and add, and on top of that, we are in America, where everything should always be growing and improving, right? Not just in ministries, but in all areas. Sometimes the costs aren't fully counted as to how hard it is on people. In and of themselves, every single thing you listed here, none of them are *bad* things, they are all great things. But then, when you see all of them together, you have to ask, how do you keep your own personal heart okay during all of it?

**MARY:** During that season, too, we realized we weren't even really being deeply involved with children and their families, we were managing the structure of it all. The kids are why we got into all this in the first place. It was a tough time; things fell apart, and we left the church. Our marriage was suffering, and we were feeling broken. When you are broken and feel isolated, you have to have people in your life who love you through it all. From that season, Craig and I basically said, "God, if you can restore our lives, our hearts, our marriage, then we will go out and talk about this and be transparent about it all." We wanted to show that you didn't have to act like you had it all together. There is such a need to be authentic. So many people started asking us to share our story, and that is where *From Hectic to Healthy* came from.

**WAYNE:** And such a powerful and honest book. So, then for several years you guys are sharing your story, you're experiencing healing and joy again. Then I get this text from Craig saying, "I never thought I'd do this again, but I took a job at a church, and I'm loving it."

**MARY:** We had been through so much. We had seen so many of our friends in the same boat as well, and I think Craig thought he would continue to do his own ministry, but not be on staff at a church again. During that season, we started Empowered Living, he kept speaking and teaching. He wrote *Faith and the Modern Family*. As things were growing and going well, we were loving it, but he would say how much he missed the closeness of working with a team, investing in them. I kept having reoccurring dreams of seeing Craig back working at a church. And I remember one day I was driving to work, and I was praying out loud to God, "God, please open the door for Craig to be in church ministry again. It's his true heartbeat." And I was specific with my prayers. "God, please make it possible for him to speak on weekends, and work with families; he is so gifted in these areas, but, God, please keep it in California." *[laughing]* Because I am a licensed speech pathologist here in the state, and it's what I love. I remember Craig said, "We are not moving, and I'm not open to it until all of our kids are out of high school. I was reminded that all through our journey, it's been clearly God when a door like that opened. And I prayed boldly, "God, will you do that again? Please, in such a way that Craig and I will know it's You!"

Within two months, Venture Church in California had offered him a position with every single thing that I had been praying for. All these specific details were brought up that Craig had not even mentioned. Things that I can't even mention here, but tons of details. I would say that 2018 was the best year of our lives. Right up until December 26 when he passed, obviously. But it was so amazing, seeing God using Craig at his fullest potential again. I got to see him come alive again. I saw his excitement, but he was not the same workaholic he had been prior. He shut down at 5:00 p.m. and he was home for dinner. He held his staff to the same standard—family time was most important. He led differently. He prioritized time off and time with family, and he led his team to do that, too.

**WAYNE:** Thank you so much for sharing all of this, Mary. How amazing to see how God walked with you both even through such hard things. And how neat to see how Craig grew to where he saw the real fruit of "overworking," and the real fruit of "family first." He is discipling many even now, and you guys don't even know the reach of all the messages and books that have gone out. God is so good.

**MARY:** Yes, I was able to witness this grace in Craig now for his team that I never really saw before. There would be times when a team member was not performing well in their job, or even directly defying what he had told them to do, or not to do. He would come home and tell me about it, and I would just be like, "I can't believe that, you need to let them go, you don't need to put up with that!" He would say, "I think I'm going to go back and talk to them again." He would give them second chances and third chances. Or he would say, "Maybe I'll just try moving them to this other position because maybe I have them in the wrong spot, and that's the reason they aren't leading well." I saw such grace in him. Whereas, before he would have just fired them. But he was looking at other things going on in their lives currently, or in their past, looking at all of it. I can remember at one point looking at him and going, "Oh my gosh, my husband is so much more like Jesus than I am. He is so much more loving and patient and forgiving." I remember thinking, *He is like Jesus!* Who says that about their spouse? Believe me, there were many times I didn't think that about him. But as that year went on, I saw this huge heart of compassion, because of the pain and discouragement that he went through. This spilled over into our family, too, with our kids, to go in asking questions instead of making an accusation. Let's seek to understand, let's ask questions, let's be open. He would say, "Let's be curious about what's going on with people instead of having a preset mind of what we think is going on."

I think about that final year, and I am so very thankful for it. We were so connected as a couple, as a family. To see him doing ministry again was such a blessing. It was God's gift to both of us. For Craig to have his final year at a church where he was valued and appreciated, all of his gifts came into play.

We look at it and say, "How, at fifty-three, can a healthy person have a heart attack?" It seems so untimely. But at the same time, you can look at all that God did through Craig's life. God also provided us a church family during this time of grieving loss. Craig was also home from 2007 to 2017, ten years. He worked from home; he was so involved with our kids' lives; he was the one driving them to school. He was all in on soccer, and swim meets, and basketball. He would take one of the kids each time if he traveled to speak. And honestly, he most likely would not have had all that time if he was still working at Saddleback. I look at that and I totally believe that God is sovereign. When we are in the pit of despair, He says, "I'm going to turn this into a valuable blessing." "The battle is mine," says the Lord. He says, "You stand still and watch me work." And what should our response be? It should be worship, to say, "Thank you!" I am learning this over and over.

Then Mary said, "Hey, I want to show you something." She picked up her laptop and moved to another part of the room to show me something on the wall. "This is Craig's story board. This is exactly how he had it the day he passed away. He was in the middle of writing a book, *7 Habits of an Emotionally Healthy Family*. I'm hoping that I will be able to one day finish that.

**WAYNE:** Beautiful. Thank you so very much, Mary, for taking the time to chat and allowing me to hear your heart and a bit more of y'all's story. It means so much.

**MARY:** I was just curious, do you have that final text that Craig sent to you? I'd love to hear it. I'm pretty sure whatever it was that he was encouraging you.

So, I shared this text thread with her:

**WAYNE:** Update me on you, bro! I'm so proud of my two little girls who are growing super fast. We had our first day of kindergarten yesterday and it was harder on me than her! Ha. I'm doing more art these days and am loving it. Another thing that is super cool, I am having a sabbatical this year, and I'm turning fifty! So, I'll be journaling all of these conversations, and if all goes well, maybe put out a book called Epic 50 . . . It's been amazing already, all of the conversations that have happened. Talks about life, faith, art . . . We'll see what happens with it. And, yes, I still play golf two to three times a year, I'm still just as bad. We need to go play again.

**CRAIG:** First day of kindergarten was hard on me, too. And the first day of his last day of college (this year) is equally hard. I LOVE the Epic50 idea! Put me on the list as an early reader. Glad the art is going well! I think I remember you telling me you really wanted to lean into that more, yes? Our boys are twenty-one, and our daughter is twenty. Can't believe it! I started a job back in a church after I said I would never go back into a church. Working at Venture Church in the Bay Area of California. Family/Next Gen and Teaching Pastor with Chip Ingram. It's going incredibly well! I'll be in Houston soon, lets connect . . . and when I come out, we have to dust off the clubs and play at least eighteen.

**MARY:** Awe. Thank you for sharing that with me; that's cool. Okay, when this book is done, I want to be an early reader, too!

Then we prayed together.

I will close with this. In December of 2018, when I found out what had happened with Craig, it really hit me hard. It made no sense at all. I remember watching his two online memorial services, both happening in California. I watched as people shared funny stories about Craig, heartfelt moments they'd had together, and touching interactions with him. The churches at both events were packed. What blew me away the most was watching the number of people from around the country and around the world who were watching the livestream. I saw the number go from 280 to 320, 320 to 390, 390 to 450, and 450 to 580. I thought, *Oh my goodness, look at all the lives that were truly impacted and changed by Craig's life!*

I want so desperately to live a life of significance, one that has taken the path to be a blessing to others.

It's my firm belief that God wants to take the giftings, abilities, and dreams we have and multiply them in ways that we can't even imagine.

So proud of you, Craig and Mary.

# THE TALE OF TWO MUSTANGS
## part two

Let me interrupt the flow of things here for a second. We need to check back in with our mustang.

Last we heard, he had jumped the wall and sprinted into a world of new adventures to join the wild herd. He experienced what it was like to run and splash through mountain streams and to feel the cold water on his back. He saw endless amounts of golden sunsets slowly closing each day over vast fields and valleys. He experienced the unknown and exhilarating feeling of running at full speed with his new herd. He was happy. He was exploring and living a wild and free life.

But remember, there was another mustang in our story.

One fall day, the wild herd had meandered its way through a rich apple orchard. That day, they each ate more apples than they could even count. To say they were happy was an understatement. The (now) wild mustang started to get a feeling that somehow the area looked strangely familiar. As they came over a hill, he saw something. He was now aware of exactly where he was.

He saw the stone wall he had jumped over just three years ago.

He also saw in the distance that same old familiar cart heading down the road. His ears perked up and he recognized the sound instantly; it was the *clack clack clack* of the cart and hooves on the road. And the crack of the whip from the same driver. Even at a distance, he recognized the other mustang who he had pulled with all those years. His old friend was still at it, making daily deliveries of lumber, but now with a new partner at his side.

The wild mustang wanted to get a closer look at his former life. He ran down toward the wall to get a better look right where the road makes the turn from the forest. As he ran, he had mixed emotions in his heart. For sure, there was a certain joy for the freedom that he now experienced. But it was also tempered with an unusual feeling of missing the routine of his former life and his mustang friend. He often missed the warm and dry barn, too, especially on the cold mountain nights with snow and freezing rain.

He found a good spot under a grove of aspen trees. This way, he could watch as they went by, but he could also hide a bit under all of the brightly colored leaves. As the cart jostled by, he saw his old friend and noticed he looked a tad older, and a bit slower, too. Our wild mustang even had the thought of trying some clever way to get his old friend to escape and come join his new life. Many times over these months, he had thought of his old friend and had often felt sorry for him. But as the team went by, he noticed something—his friend had a proud look in his eyes.

Mustangs aren't especially known for their facial expressions, either, but he sure looked happy. After the cart flew by, and the dust settled, our wild mustang turned and noticed that the little town had grown. A lot. There were new buildings and people everywhere.

As the cart and team pulled over to stop and unload, the wild mustang could now see why his old friend seemed so proud. His daily delivery of lumber over all this time had been used to build what was now a growing community. There was a schoolhouse for the children, a mercantile, a boardwalk, and even a new church building. They were now dropping off a load of lumber for what would become the new doctor's office.

A true sense of peace came over our wild mustang friend. He realized that just as he was following his heart to remain a wild mustang, his friend had actually been following his own heart, too. He was playing a huge role in changing the lives of all those human types, for the better. In those moments as he looked at the town, he realized his friend was doing what he loved with his life. He had no need to jump over the wall to pursue something different. He loved pulling the cart and delivering wood to the builders and craftsmen.

Within a few minutes, the cart and team had unloaded and turned around. The wild mustang thought to run off before they came by but realized it was too late. Best bet was to stay frozen under the leaves and pretend that he was a statue. As the team passed by the stone wall, the driver could have sworn he saw something that looked just like a horse with a brightly colored aspen leaf-type mane, but he dismissed it to a bad breakfast.

As the team came by, the mustang made eye contact with our hiding friend. He had seen the wild mustang earlier and was in no way surprised. He wanted his friend to know that he was happy for him in his new wild adventurous life. He also hoped that his now wild friend could see that he, too, was content and joyful in his own life. In that brief moment that went by like a blur, both mustangs looked at each other, arched their heads back, proudly stuck out their chests, and did something that mustangs don't often do.

They winked at each other.

I hope that my allegory about the two mustangs speaks something to you. A good allegory, from what I understand, paints a picture that can reveal a hidden meaning. I hope that in some way you can see yourself in the story. Do you? If you do, which mustang are you? In fact, I'm reminded that I am often a little bit of each of them. In different seasons of life, either mustang's story might resonate with us.

There is value in working hard over a lifetime at a certain job, or on a certain dream. For the mustang who didn't break free, his story of braving meant that he loved to work hard for his master and haul the lumber. For weeks, months, and years he labored and helped make a literal difference in the community. His heart was content to be who he was created to be. His heart was full. Over the course of his life, he gave his best. The word "meraki" sure comes to mind.

For the wild mustang, his heart thrived in the open wild. His story of braving meant overcoming his fear and jumping into the unknown to be wild. For weeks, months, and years he explored, ran, and did what wild mustangs do. His heart was content to be who he was created to be. His heart was full.

Each mustang was wired differently, and that's okay.

Each of us are wired differently. Thank goodness. Not only is this okay, but it's amazing!

You are wired to be you. In fact, we all *need* you to be you.

You can be *brave*, and yes, your heart can thrive.

# SOME THINGS TO KICK AROUND

1. In what ways are you feeling tempted to run after success instead of significance?

_____

_____

_____

_____

_____

2. Why not only strive for success?

_____

_____

_____

_____

_____

3. Here is how I will apply "Significance versus Success" to my life, starting now:

_____

_____

_____

_____

_____

*chapter seven*

# BE PRESENT, BE THANKFUL

"Treasure is measured in units of love
Which means you may find
You are rich beyond your wildest dreams."

—"Treasure," Above and Beyond

Read the lyrics of the epigraph above again, slowly, staying fully present in the moment. What comes to your mind when you are reading them? More importantly, *who* comes to mind? Who can you be thankful for right now?

A theme that has come up so often during these interviews has been having a thankful heart. Seriously, it has been like a bell that keeps going off in these conversations. Another theme that kept circling back around was needing to be fully present. Here are a few of the most powerful interviews that I've had so far.

# JOHNNY CARRABBA

"When I got my first rough copy of the book, I was on a flight from here to New York. In the book, there are pictures of any employees that have been with me fifteen years or longer. Literally, I cried from the time I opened the book when we took off, to the time we landed. That's probably a three-hour flight. It was so emotional for me."

John Charles Carrabba III, y'all! He is a fellow Houstonian and an amazing guy! If you love Italian food, you have probably eaten at one of the over 220 Carrabba's restaurants in America and abroad. It was a huge joy and honor to connect with Johnny at his original location in Houston.

I will say I felt like I was an actor in a super cool Italian movie from the 1970s when I went to meet with Johnny. I was a few minutes early when I arrived at his restaurant. Many employees were there working, getting ready to open up for lunch. There was not a single person in the place other than the staff and me. A gentleman greeted me at the door.

"Are you here to meet with Johnny?"

"Yes, sir." I said.

"Please wait in here, he usually likes to meet with people here in the blue room."

"Wow, this is amazing!" I said to myself. (I think I said it out loud). The blue room is sick, y'all. The walls are covered with black and white photos of Italian singers, actors and actresses, as well as amazing history of the restaurant in Houston. I strolled around for a minute or two looking at this beautiful restaurant. If you have not been to the original location on Kirby Dr. in Houston, do yourself a favor and go! On one wall I saw an official document hung under glass in a nice frame. The mayor of Houston had just a few years ago appointed and declared "Carrabba's Day" on the thirtieth anniversary of the opening of the first restaurant. The document read:

"In December of 1986, the original Carrabba's opened its doors to the public. It had seven bar stools, a main dining room, and a small prep kitchen. There was nothing over $10, the wine list was slim, but still it was a hit. Its success was due to its fantastic food, comfort, and mature servers and employees who knew the customers by name. Carrabba's success stems from uncompromising high standards that don't go out of style."

My first experience with Johnny in person came the previous year. For the past ten or so years, I've been blessed with the opportunity to share at chapel once a year with the students of River Oaks Baptist School. This is an amazing school with incredible kids and teachers. Last year, when I was there to do some music and speak, they let me know that Johnny Carrabba would be there as well to make a presentation. Come to find out, it was a scholarship that he was awarding the school, not to the kids, but to the teachers! I sat there in awe as he shared his heart, not only for the school, but for the teachers there. Teachers were chosen (by a team of students) to receive higher education and training. Some involved incredible trips to amazing places, like studying art in Italy for the art teacher. You should have seen the look on the faces of the teachers that were chosen. *Wow, this guy is truly giving back and investing in people*, I thought.

I remember him saying to the kids, "Always be thankful, have a thankful heart. Today when your parents come pick you up at the end of the day, you need to say, 'Thank you for making sacrifices so I can get an education like this!'" He went on, "Wherever you go in life, wherever it takes you, have a thankful heart, and you will succeed."

When it came time to work on this book and look at the topic of thankfulness, Johnny came to mind. It was a blessing and honor to hang out with him and have our conversation—in the blue room.

**WAYNE:** You talk often about the culture of your employees, many of whom have been working with you for twenty, even thirty years. Incredible. These folks are like your family, right?

**JOHNNY:** For sure. This is my family. This gives me more joy than you could imagine. I did a cookbook a few years ago. It was our thirtieth anniversary, and the experts that were helping us put the book together said they needed to have my picture on the front of it. I said, "No way, this is not what it's about. This is a thirty-year celebration that I want to give to my good friends and customers." The title of the book is *With Gratitude.* I don't think that people show enough gratitude. I could never thank the community here enough for what they have done for me. And I for sure can't thank my people that work here with me enough.

When I got my first rough copy of the book, I was on a flight from here to New York. In the book, there are pictures of any employees that have been with me fifteen years or longer. Literally, I cried from the time I opened the book when we took off, to the time we landed. That's probably a three-hour flight. It was so emotional for me.

**WAYNE:** That was so cool how you presented scholarships to some of those teachers. Tell me how that came to be.

**JOHNNY:** I was raised by my grandparents and my parents, and they were giving souls. They were mainly merchants and were immigrants. They were selfless. They gave up all their time to their family. I give for the sake of giving, not for the sake of gaining. Those teachers . . . by teaching, they are not becoming millionaires, they are dedicating their lives to what they love doing, and I wanted them to benefit. They are investing in the next generation.

**WAYNE:** What's a crazy or fun story from your years of running the restaurant here?

**JOHNNY:** Pretty much every day around here is hilarious. I pride myself on hiring characters, so my staff, they crack me up on a daily basis. Let's see, some of the days I've really loved . . . like Billy Gibbons of ZZ Top. He would call me at 10 o'clock at night, and say, "I know you're closing up, but is there any way we can come in? We are in the studio working late."

"Sure," I'd say. They would stay here till like 5 o'clock in the morning and pay our staff tons extra. Those were fun days.

**WAYNE:** How did you decide your career path when you were younger?

**JOHNNY:** I had an uncle of mine, Uncle Ciro. When I was graduating from high school he said to me, "Hey, Johnny, what are you gonna do with yourself after you graduate?"

I said, "I'm gonna go to college and be an accountant."

He goes, "Really? I can't see you being an accountant."

"Well it's one of my better grades, and I enjoy it. Plus, I have a friend of mine, his dad is an accountant, and he makes a lot of money . . ."

My uncle stopped me in my tracks and said, "Hey, boy. You never do something for the money. You do something because you love it, and the money will follow. He reminded me that what I loved was being with people, and the restaurant business was something I was learning to love—the people.

**WAYNE:** Your uncle sounded pretty amazing. Seems as if you had quite a few older folks speaking into your life when you were young.

**JOHNNY:** I always tell young people that I learned a lot from my coaches and teachers. But when I really look back on my journey, I've learned a lot from older people. It's good to talk to them; old people have that fail rate—they've failed, they've learned. I admire young people that reach out to older people. Sometimes young people want instant success, instant gratification. There's no easy way. These days you can almost learn anything from your phone, like how to cook. But when you look at the best cooks, in my opinion, they are people like my grandmothers. It was trial and error. You put your time in to refine your craft.

**WAYNE:** True success doesn't just happen, much less overnight.

**JOHNNY:** Often, people really know that with success comes pain and agony. It's like running a marathon, not that I would know, ha-ha! But I have run a half-marathon. And when you are in the middle of it, it's like every step can be brutal, but when you reach the end, you look back and relish in the work that was put in to reach your goal. I have such a heart for young people, and I love investing in them and helping them learn these things. There was an old saying that an old waiter, Bubba, told me, he said, "It's nice to be important, but it's more important to be nice." At this stage in my life I want to be a giver. It's too exhausting to try and be someone else, or to keep up with what other people are achieving. I just want to be me, I'm totally okay with being me.

**WAYNE:** What advice would you give to someone who is wanting to go for it—the adventure of their life?

**JOHNNY:** I tell my children this all the time. It's what young people need to understand. They shouldn't do things just because they think it's expected of them. My dad is a doctor, so I need to be a doctor. I think everyone would expect my kids would get in the restaurant business. But I've been telling my children since they were little, "I don't care what you do. If you want to be a fishing guide, a social worker, whatever you want to be—just do it to the best of your ability! More importantly, do something that you love."

The other thing, I have another uncle, his name was Rocco. Can you imagine being Italian and having an Uncle Ciro and Uncle Rocco? But Uncle Rocco used to tell me, "Knowledge is very powerful, because knowledge gives you a wonderful thing that's called confidence." When you know you can make the shot, when you know you can strum the chord, or whatever we do . . . for me, cooking. If I have that knowledge, it's going to give me confidence. He said the most important word to live by is "enthusiasm." If you have the knowledge, which builds the confidence, and you throw enthusiasm on that? That's an unbeatable combination.

**WAYNE:** What other things have you learned along your journey?

**JOHNNY:** Matthew McConaughey has an amazing message on happiness. He talks about how happiness is a moving target. You know you're happy today, not tomorrow, and it's elusive. Then he talked about joy. Joy is something different. This speech really spoke to me, because sometimes in business you get wrapped up. Like, "Hey I wanna have ten restaurants in this amount of time, do this many dollars in a certain time, then sell it." And honestly, whenever I start thinking like that, I lose my joy. He said when he doesn't focus on the "needing a blockbuster," but on the art, he'd have so much joy! Kind of like with my business, what gives me joy is being here with my people. Grooming somebody to be better at what they do; that comes with age, I think. I enjoy giving. I enjoy making people happy.

This is what happened to me. I kept on wanting to grow the Mia's restaurants I have. I kept having a number in my head. I thought I wanted to open up twelve Mia's restaurants (my daughter's name is Mia). I kept focusing so much on that. Then one day I finally realized I was like a mouse running in the wheel! I realized, that's not me. I don't want things to always be bigger. I want to have family-owned restaurants with that positive culture. It was just a few months ago when I had this revelation. It doesn't matter . . . I'm happy, probably happier. Every time that I venture out too far from that, it's like I get too thin, and I realize I'm getting off track.

There was a great baseball player, Joe DiMaggio, who played for the New York Yankees. Joe said he played the game of baseball hard every single play. In my life, nine banks turned me down for my first Carrabba's. The tenth bank came from a recommendation from a customer that I had. Then, the banker that he sent me to, she happened to be a customer that I didn't know. One of the founders of Outback Steakhouse who took Carrabba's across the country, he happened to be a customer that I didn't know. So, you never know. Play the game hard. Be proud of what you do. Give your best.

**WAYNE:** You were planting seeds and not trying to angle to get to the right people.

**JOHNNY:** Yes, you see, that's what I don't like. A lot of people give for the sake of gaining. Real givers give for the sake of giving, not to get something in return. I got a text message the other day from a doctor, and it said, "I just want to congratulate you for what you've done with your restaurant. My dad had his leg amputated six months ago. My sister brought him in the restaurant and your staff took him into the restroom and helped him out. What a great culture." And I was reminded yet again, it's not about the money. It's not about how many restaurants I have. It's what gives me joy, making people happy. It's all about relationships. I have a friend, his wife just passed away. He was actually my very first customer. I served food at the celebration for her life. He called me up and said, "Johnny, you're not in the restaurant business, you're in the love business." And that is something that now we tell our staff all the time, "We are in the love business."

At the end of our time together, he displayed his giving heart again. He gave me a copy of his book. When I left, I sat in my truck for a few minutes and looked through the pages. Not only was the recipe for Chicken Bryan in there, thank you *Lord*, but I saw picture after picture after picture of his employees. The love is real. It's not every company or organization that has employees stay around for twenty- or thirty-plus years. Incredible. I want to be a cheerful giver like Johnny. I want to be present and do my best in the moment, and to have a thankful heart like Johnny.

# MARK HARRIS

> "The best thing, though, was my decision to coach baseball that year. My son, who is grown now, says that he doesn't remember too much from ages five to eleven when his dad was a part-time, kinda-there, assistant coach. But he totally remembers being twelve, when his dad was the head coach of his team. Every practice. Every game. I was present."

Mark is a singer-songwriter and worship leader. For sixteen years, he was with the group *4Him*. Back in the day, they had several hits, "The Basics of Life" being one of my favs! These guys won like ten Dove Awards, had Grammy nominations, and had multiple gold records. Mark currently serves as the worship pastor at Gateway Church in the Dallas area. It was super cool to get to chat with him. As I was putting my list together of who I would love to connect with, Mark was one of the first people on my mind. The list of people who did traveling music ministry (like I did), write their own songs, and then navigated a big transition into a second chapter, or career even, is kind of a short list. As with many of these interviews I did, I was like a kid who was super jazzed to connect with someone they look up to! Mark and I met for lunch in Dallas.

**WAYNE:** Tell me how the transition happened between you being in *4Him* as a group, and starting the next chapter in your life. Basically, how did you know it was time to wrap it up?

**MARK:** My son had just turned twelve. He loved baseball, and I was basically a part-time assistant coach on his team. I came to practices and games whenever we weren't on the road touring. I remember the day that he asked me to be the head coach of his team. He said, "Dad, you know more about baseball than the other coaches, and plus I like it better when you are there."

Mark went on to tell me the story of how that gripped his heart, and how he knew he would never get this time back.

**MARK:** I remember we had a meeting a few weeks later with the *4Him* team, the band guys, manager, and label folks, and I told them that the following spring I was going to be coaching my son's baseball team. And that basically meant I could not be out on the road on Tuesdays, Thursday, or Saturdays.

**WAYNE:** How did that go over?

**MARK:** Obviously, they all looked at me a bit shocked. When our tours would normally go out, it would be for two weeks at a time. It would be kind of hard to be only available on Fridays and Sundays. I told them we could do one-off performances, and that I could make any fly dates, as long as it didn't interfere with my son's team. Our manager called me into his office a few days later and asked if I'd really thought through how this would impact the other three guys, their livelihoods, and their families. Not to mention, the other people on that team and the record label. I knew it was a huge decision, but God wouldn't leave me alone about it. Also, a few of the other guys in *4Him* were feeling the time was right also to start to step back. So prayerfully, the decision was made.

**WAYNE:** What a big life moment that was. I guess some decisions in life are the small ones, this one was huge! So how did things go that spring?

**MARK:** The time was right. We did do several dates that spring, but it was more or less the beginning of the end of *4Him* and that season for all of us. The best thing, though, was my decision to coach baseball that year. My son, who is grown now, says that he doesn't remember too much from ages five to eleven, when his dad was a part-time, kinda-there assistant coach. But he totally remembers being twelve, when his dad was the head coach of his team. Every practice. Every game. I was present.

**WAYNE:** In a time of making a decision like that, whether it be a life-change-sized one, or a smaller, day-to-day decision, what helps you know which road to take?

**MARK:** I pray! I'm going to follow peace. Look, here's my question I ask of someone who is at a crossroads or thinking of starting something new. If it's 3:00 a.m. and you wake up in the middle of the night, are you worried about your future in that direction, or are you excited about it? That's telling you a lot.

Mark and I spent the next hour or two just chatting and sharing stories. This story I want to share with you impacted me. It continues to make an impression on me daily.

**MARK:** Wayne, I think its cool what you are doing. Not only the aspect of connecting with so many people from different walks of life, but the fact that you're fifty, and taking the time to pause and evaluate is good. A friend of mine told me a story when he was asking some of the same questions.

He was boarding a flight and took his seat when an elderly man sat down next to him. He was frail and moving slowly. My friend wanted to know more about his story, wanted to chat with the man, but shortly after takeoff, the man dozed off. A little over an hour later, the plane started its descent. The attendants came around and asked people to prepare for landing, and they woke the gentleman up for the touchdown that was coming shortly.

My friend asked the man, "Are you traveling alone?"

"Yes," the man answered.

"Will there be anyone to meet you when we land?" my friend asked, honestly a little worried about him.

"Oh yes, someone is picking me up."

"If you don't mind me asking you, sir, how old are you?"

"I'm ninety-seven."

"Wow, that's amazing. Could I ask you one more question before we land? I turned fifty a few weeks ago, and I'm wondering, what would you, at ninety-seven, tell your fifty-year-old self?" my friend asked.

The man replied, "Oh, that's easy, I can show you right here." He reached into his pants pocket and pulled out a golf marker, almost like a poker chip, that had something printed on each side. On one side of the marker it said, "Be Present." On other side of the marker it said, "Be Thankful."

The man shared the meaning behind it. "When I was younger, I was a very successful business man. I had my hands in several companies and was always on the go. If I was at a lunch meeting, I wasn't really at the lunch meeting, my mind was thinking about the 3 o'clock phone call I'd be on. During the 3 o'clock call, I'd have all the right answers and ideas, but my mind was already on to the next thing. At dinner, I wasn't really at dinner, my mind was racing about the proposal I needed to type up, and so on. This is how I got ahead. People praised me as the guy who always had the right answers. People always applauded how ahead of the game I was.

He went on, "I was consumed with work and getting ahead. We had five children. Two of them have already passed away, and the other three, I have no relationship with them."

Then the plane touched down.

Oh, that I might be present. That I might be thankful. This story messed me up. Bless that man's heart, but I don't want to be him when I look back on my own life. I don't know about you, but what is the point of achieving and achieving, if all that is left in your wake is the wreckage of your family and those you love?

Let me put it this way. What would I want my epitaph to say? What will they put on my gravestone when this short time is over?

What will yours say?

Morgan Snyder, who does the podcast *Become Good Soil*, shared this quote. It was the potential wording for his tombstone one day. It is the wording that he is determined will NOT be there.

HE CAME THROUGH. PROUDLY AND ANXIOUSLY, FOR MANY AND FOR MUCH, AT THE EXPENSE OF WHO AND WHAT MATTERED MOST.[16]

Since hearing this story from Mark, I've shared it with many people. I got to speak at my home church after my sabbatical was over, and this was a key element to the message. In fact, we printed 2,000 wristbands that said, "Be Present, Be Thankful." All of them were gone at the end of service. We've had to order more.

I was in Ruidoso, New Mexico last summer, and I was picking up some food to-go. While I was sitting at a table in this restaurant, I noticed a family sitting across from me. The dad and mom looked to be in their mid-twenties, the little boy six or so, and little girl maybe four. Dad was staring at his phone, scrolling through some feed. Mom was staring at her phone, scrolling through some feed. Both were probably looking at other people's lives, when their life was right there in front of them. Both kids were trying to angle for their attention, trying to compete, then giving up, then trying again. Then they finally gave up.

Wreckage comes slowly sometimes.

Lord, help us to be *present* and to be *thankful.*

Lord, help me to be *present* and to be *thankful.*

My friend Dan Payne, who plays drums with me sometimes on the road, is a super cool guy. He is a body builder, a drummer, a baseball coach, a husband, and a soon-to-be realtor. He has a huge tattoo sleeve covering his entire arm. After I shared this story with him, he said he is considering getting a new tattoo. "Be Present" on his left thumb. On the hand that holds his cell phone. The cell phone that competes daily, hourly, and moment-by-moment for his attention.

There are dreams I hope to achieve. BIG ones. I think that you have some, too. Or else you would not have picked up this book with the title *Braving.* You can achieve more than you imagine. With God's help, all things are truly possible! But don't sacrifice what matters most to get to it.

King Solomon spent seven years building the great temple and thirteen years building his palace. After he did all that, here's what he had to say:

> I made great works. I built houses and planted vineyards for myself. I made myself gardens and parks, and planted in them all kinds of fruit trees. I made myself pools from which to water the forest of growing trees. I bought male and female slaves, and had slaves who were born in my house. I had also great possessions of herds and flocks, more than any who had been before me in Jerusalem. I also gathered for myself silver and gold and the treasure of kings and provinces. I got singers, both men and women, and many concubines, the delight of the sons of man.
>
> So I became great and surpassed all who were before me in Jerusalem. Also my wisdom remained with me. And whatever my eyes desired I did not keep from them. I kept my heart from no pleasure,

for my heart found pleasure in all my toil, and this was my reward for all my toil. Then I considered all that my hands had done and the toil I had expended in doing it, and behold, all was vanity and a striving after wind, and there was nothing to be gained under the sun.

—ECCLESIASTES 2:4–11 (ESV)

# DEBBIE BROWNE

"I grew up in a generation in the 60s and 70s where it became all about us and our rights, and whatever felt good to us at the time. It didn't matter if we hurt anybody else. In my late teens it became all about how to serve me, and it was an empty life. It was one that was never happy or fulfilled. It wasn't until I started giving back that I started experiencing real joy."

I received an email one day requesting a commissioned painting. It was from a lady who had picked up my card out at the Round Top Antiques Fair, where I had an art booth. Her email mentioned she would like to see if I'd be open to doing a piece for her, a large one. I'll be honest, sometimes if people reach out to me for commissions, you never know what they are going to ask for. It may be a picture of their cat, a parrot, who knows what.

She sent me the images of what she might want painted, and I was blown away. They were pictures of her when she was like nine years old, dressed up in a cowgirl outfit. Her hat was down close to her eyes, gun drawn, as if she was defending her doll that was on the ground. Her face of almost sheer defiance seemed to say, "Come and take it." When I saw these photos, I knew I was in, and that this painting was going to be epic. I completed the large painting for her, and it now hangs in her Austin, Texas condo above her living room sofa. High up on the twenty-fourth floor, this is a centerpiece for conversation. It would be the centerpiece for the conversation we had as well. I named the painting, "Don't Mess with Mama!"

During the weeks of communicating back and forth on her piece, it became clear that this lady had quite a story to tell. I'm thrilled to include her here in this log of my *Braving* conversations. She has overcome much, and is inspiring many, many people today. She is an author in her own right and a public speaker. She oversees a ministry that reaches out to, encourages, and inspires families walking through the illness of Turner Syndrome. I had not even heard of Turner Syndrome before we met. You'll read more about her story here, in the transcript of our conversation in Austin. What a complete blessing to share it with you.

**WAYNE:** Tell me your story, Debbie, about the journey you've been on.

**DEBBIE:** I grew up in a Christian family that was mission-oriented. We helped support mission workers around the world. I had always felt, even as a little girl, that I was called into some sort of missions, to help people, to reach out to people in some way. But I didn't think it meant me going to the jungle somewhere, but that seed was planted. Fast-forward into my adult years. I got a little disillusioned with organized church, and how some people were treating each other. I went off the rails a little bit in the 1970s. But God even used those situations to prepare me for where I am today.

I saw a clear picture of what life looked like without God versus life with God. Then I found myself as a woman in her twenties with two preschoolers. I joined a ladies' Bible study because I realized I didn't know anything about the Bible, even though I grew up in church. I look back, and I can easily see every step of how God prepared me for where I am now.

When my daughter Kellie was diagnosed at the age of five with Turner Syndrome, I'll admit I looked at it as some sort of punishment toward me. I began to struggle with questions like: What do I do with this diagnosis? Why had this happened? Who else in the world has this? At that point I'd never even heard of it.

**WAYNE:** And yes, back in the day, it wasn't like you could just Google a bunch of information on Turner Syndrome and get answers quickly.

**DEBBIE:** Exactly. In 1984, there was no information highway, no support groups for something like this. I just put it in the closet. I thought God will heal her— she's smart, doing great in school. But she went on to battle much, and by the age of twenty-eight was battling major heart issues because of this. I was able to have a very precious three months with her. Even when she was in the ICU, there were several beautiful days when she had to be completely still due to her heart. Together we listened to worship music; we prayed for the doctors and nurses. When they would walk in, we would ask, "How can we pray for you?" Even in this challenging time, it was a beautiful time for Kellie and me. I am so thankful for that time. We lost her in 2008. At that time, she had a double major in college, was a fifth-grade teacher, and was about to get married. *Why now?* I wondered.

After she passed away, and the grief began to subside, then the "what" instead of the "why" began to come up. *What am I going to do with this? Am I going to do what my mother did when her mother died?* She went into a room, drew the shade, and slept for months. No, I can't do that.

"I began to look around outside of myself and found a whole world out there of people who were dealing with Turner Syndrome. An entire community that involved moms, dads, grandparents, siblings, and friends. There are over 80,000 girls and women in the United States dealing with Turners. What was I going to do with this information, because once you learn something, how do you unlearn it?

For some reason, I felt like God had called me to write a book about this. I thought, *Hey, You have the wrong person here!* I realized that He wrote the book through me, because now this book is reaching people all over the world. I have met families in Hungary, Australia, Canada, all over the place. That's only because they contacted me after they read the book. I then saw that I had just reached the tip of the iceberg. I realized this was a ministry that I was called to.

**WAYNE:** So powerful, Debbie. God is using your story and Kellie's story to reach out to and minster to so many who are currently walking through this.

**DEBBIE:** It's unreal. We have spiritual retreats, we talk with people, pray with people, love them. It has been so very healing. We think somehow we can do something to help other people, and it ends up helping us.

**WAYNE:** I'm thinking of what you said a bit ago, even as a little girl you wanted to help other people, but in some ways you were scared to go around the world. Look at how God is bringing people from around the world to you, to connect with you. He is bringing flowers out of the ashes.

**DEBBIE:** I'm a very visual person. So, when I saw the number—80,000— representing how many girls are dealing with this in our nation alone, I realized, wow, that is a huge stadium filled with precious girls and women. And this is just them, not the families and communities affected. This is my outreach to meet them where they are.

**WAYNE:** What would be your challenge to anyone reading this story right now?

**DEBBIE:** I am currently writing my second book. The first one was our story. This second one will be their stories. The last chapter will be called "Surrender." My question is, "What are you going to do with your 'whys' to turn them into what you can do to make a difference. Because it's very healing to do that.

**WAYNE:** Thank you, Debbie, so much for sharing your heart. Some things we do are huge and some things may seem small, but they might make a huge impact. I was at an event in Houston last week celebrating an organization that teaches English to hundreds of refugees. It was a fun outreach with food and games, families and kids were everywhere. My job that day was at the jump rope station. So, there I stood holding one side of the jump rope as kids one at a time took a turn. As I watched this little five-year-old girl wearing a hijab jump with a huge smile on her face, I realized it. This is the small thing I can do today. I can smile at her, and let her jump rope for a little bit.

Then, at that same event they asked if anyone had a large vehicle to go pick up the pizzas. I volunteered, as I have a truck. I had *no idea* that it was ninety pizzas! But they all fit, and I realized, I have an empty truck, so I'll make it available in some small way. Maybe my big calling on being there that day wasn't anything more than just being available to do some jump rope and get some pizzas for families. But I know in my heart everyone's small offerings add up, and just might be huge in someone's life. And, if I'm honest, I kind of didn't want to go that day. I was behind on two projects, lots going on. I thought, *Hey, my wife and little girls can go and it'll be great.* But then I realized how very rare chances come to do things like that as a family. I'm so glad we all went.

**DEBBIE:** God only asks us to be the hands and feet, not to be the head of everything all the time.

**WAYNE:** Can I quote that? Amazing!

**DEBBIE:** Sure. I just made that up.

**WAYNE:** Okay, last question for ya. Not just in terms of the parts of your story you have shared, it can be in general. What would sixty-four-year-old Debbie tell twenty-year-old Debbie?

**DEBBIE:** Hmm . . . I will say that my grandmother and my mother were so influential on me. They used to have all these little sayings. The biggest one was, "You can't outgive God." I think many people have heard something like that, but I would tell my twenty-year-old self this. I'd remind myself to not be so self-centered. I grew up in a generation in the 60s and 70s where it became all about us and our rights, and whatever felt good to us at the time. It didn't matter if we hurt anybody else. In my late teens, it became all about how to serve me, and it was an empty life. It was one where I never felt happy or fulfilled. It wasn't until I started giving back that I started experiencing real joy.

**WAYNE:** It's interesting you say that about the 60s and 70s. But that mentality is even more so now. This is the generation of "I." The iPhone. My own social media existence, my universe that revolves around me. Still, for every generation, all the way to Adam and Eve, it's always been about "I." It's in our human DNA. No one had to teach my little girls at age one to say "mine."

Thank you, Debbie, so much for sharing your story, your heart. Thank you for taking the sweet life of your daughter and multiplying the love you have for her to reach hundreds and thousands around the world. Thank you for reminding people of the importance of cherishing the moment and being thankful.

Debbie's ministry is called Leaping Butterfly. Kellie died on leap year day in 2008. Debbie says that "Butterflies don't leap, but she knows one who did."

# ASHLEY FERGUSON

Ashley and her family own and manage Marburger Farm. It's a fun and unique venue in Round Top, Texas. This 43-acre property full of old buildings and awesomeness is only open for two shows per year and has been running since 1997. I mentioned the Round Top Antiques Festival earlier in the book; it's an epic event. If you ever get a chance to come down to Texas for this, you should do it. At Marburger alone there are 180 vendors from around the country. I've been blessed to be a part of this event. There is amazing food, incredible people, and treasures to find. I caught up with Ashley in Marburger to hear more of her story.

**WAYNE**: What's your favorite thing about this show? What's your favorite thing about running all this craziness?

**ASHLEY**: It's the community, the people. It's a ton of work, but when the shows actually get off and running, it's amazing. I get to sit back and watch all these vendors reconnect with each other every six months, and it's like watching mini-camp reunions going on. As you know, Wayne, as a vendor here yourself, this is hard work. It's not easy to take a 43-acre cow pasture and turn it into a wonderland. These vendors that come from all over the country, they are working hard, but they are not just doing it for the money, they continue to return because of the experience. Seeing how people help each other out, it's so amazing. From the gate crew, to porters, to the dealers, to the shoppers, it's all so special. Things like watching the grandmothers, daughters, and granddaughters who do family trips out here every six months is so meaningful. We've watched some of these kiddos grow up before our eyes. So yes, definitely the people and the relationships are my favorite. You are talking about being thankful—I am hugely grateful for these precious relationships.

**WAYNE**: What's one of the craziest or funniest stories from working out here?

**ASHLEY**: I don't know, there are so many things! I think it's crazy when we see these well-known people come through the gate. Like famous people, stars in their own right, coming through the gate, paying $10 just like everyone else, going to park where everyone parks—it's wild. They won't tell us they are coming, they don't want any special treatment, they just love coming for the experience. That's really cool. That's really my goal with all this, is to create an experience. We want to create an oasis in the middle of all the craziness in life. We want people to just walk in and go, "Hey, this place is different."

**WAYNE:** So now you guys are twelve years along on doing this show. A lot has changed in the world in that time. There was no social media in 2007. How were you guys getting the word out? A lot has changed, as this show has exploded!

**ASHLEY:** This is my twenty-second show here. And, no, there was no social media going on. We were mailing out 50,000 cards every show. Now we mail nothing. When we started this show in 2007, there were twenty shows in this area, now there are over eighty-five. So, we are constantly thinking and working on ways to improve and make this a great experience for people. But, at the same time, it's really about fostering the relationships we have with people.

**WAYNE:** How is it juggling all of this, balancing a large bi-annual event that has staff and volunteers, and being a mom and a wife?

**ASHLEY:** I've seen how God allowed me to be stretched in all this, and to be full-on tackling this business, while at the same time working from home, which allowed me to be involved in my girls' day-to-day lives. I don't take that for granted, and am very, very thankful. Being a mom is my number one priority. Interestingly, I've seen my girls grow to be more self-reliant, which has given them loads of confidence, which I love. One of my big prayers as we took on this business was that the girls wouldn't start to resent Marburger, because of all the time commitment it took. They are so involved, they love it, and they are my biggest cheerleaders, along with my husband, of course.

**WAYNE:** I remember a moment when I was young when my mom sat me on her knee and said, "Wayne, you can do whatever you want with your life." I remember it so very clearly. My sweet girls are now five and seven, and I try and tell them that every single day. I want them to be empowered. If you were going to say something to seven-year-old Ashley, what would you say?

**ASHLEY:** Oh wow, I would say trust in the Lord. It may not look the way you want it to look, but even in the hard is when you can fully trust in Him. I was thinking about this the other day. I'm an introvert, and often filled with doubts. My desire was never to be a business woman. My heart was to be a stay-at-home mom. But, you know what, I don't think I would be so aware of my dependence on God as I am right now if it weren't for doing all this. It stretches me so much in so many areas, areas that I'm not naturally confident in. So, I think if I'd speak to myself as a little girl, I would want to remind her that her confidence comes from the Lord, He's her protector, the protector of her reputation, her heart.

Incredible time connecting with folks like Ashley, Debbie, Mark, and Johnny. It was powerful to hear from these very successful folks that relationships are the most important thing. Their stories encourage me, and I hope they do you, too. May their desire to be fully present, and to be thankful, challenge us to do the same.

## SOME THINGS TO KICK AROUND

1. What stood out to you the most in this chapter about being present and being thankful?

_____

_____

_____

_____

_____

_____

2. Write out thirty people or things you are thankful for. Maybe even call or reach out to some of those on your list and express your thankfulness today.

_____

_____

_____

_____

_____

_____

_____

3. The tough spot for me when trying to fully be present is usually this:

_____

_____

_____

_____

_____

_____

_____

4. Here is how I will apply "Be Present, Be Thankful" to my life starting now:

_____

_____

_____

_____

_____

_____

_____

# *chapter eight*
# LIFELONG LEARNER

> "We keep moving forward, opening new doors, and doing new things, because we're curious and curiosity keeps leading us down new paths."[17]
>
> —Walt Disney

No one in my immediate family had gone to college, so the goal of graduating from high school was the main priority. I grew up in a hardworking, blue-collar family. They sacrificed much for my sister and me to be able to follow our dreams. After I graduated from high school, I just went to work wherever I could find it. During that year, I worked a lot of pretty bad jobs. Some were through a temp agency. I'd walk in one week and they would send me to a telemarketing company for a few days. The next week, I'd be sent to a huge warehouse to move boxes, in the Texas heat with no air conditioning. I tell you, nothing will inspire you to get an education like doing some intense physical labor in the hot Texas sun. It did teach me a good work ethic, though, and it taught me there is no shame in a hard day's work. After one year of that type of stuff, I was all set to get into college and pursue art.

One job I got during that season was pretty spectacular. It was at something that doesn't even exist anymore. This will completely date me as an old guy, but are you ready? I got a job at a . . .

Record store.

You know, records? Albums? CDs? MUSIC! Ha-ha!

It was only 1987, people, but it seems like a million years ago. When I think about it, in fact, it's kind of sad. I think of my two little girls. They won't know what it's like to walk through a record store, and to browse albums or hear music playing in the building that they've never heard before. I know there are a handful of record shops out there now that are trying to make a comeback selling LPs, but for the most part, those days are gone, y'all. Now music is streamed onto your phone. On your phone, of all things.

During this season of my life before I went off to college, I worked at Sound Warehouse in Houston, Texas. The reason that I know it was 1987 is because I remember working at the store the day the album *Joshua Tree* by U2 was released. I had kind of heard of them, but I wasn't at all ready for that happened that day. Literally *all day*, all I did was cut open big cardboard boxes full of *Joshua Tree* CDs, take them out to the floor, and stock the shelf. Within about thirty minutes, all that I had put out would be gone. I would go back, cut open another box, put them out. Repeat. By about 2:00 p.m. I was like, "Who are these guys?" That album went on to sell over 25 million copies.

I have a clear memory of one morning going into the store as part of the "opening" crew. You came in an hour before opening, swept up, made sure things were ready before they opened the doors. During open hours, the store had to play music that would drive sales, so it was like top 40, or whatever was popular. (Or U2 that year!) But in the mornings, the manager could play whatever they wanted. He would play jazz or instrumental stuff that was relaxing, because once those doors were open, the day would be crazy.

I remember so clearly pushing a broom down this aisle, when I started hearing this music. It was like a harp, with amazing melodies and sounds I'd never heard before. I stopped in the middle of the aisle and was kind of frozen. Something new was hitting me. I was basically mesmerized. The artist was Andreas Vollenweider, a musician from Switzerland. I had never heard this kind of thing before. "Andreas who?" I asked. All I knew of music was what was on one of the four radio stations at the time, or what was in the most recent hit movie. But whatever this was, it was like a door was opening in my heart to a brand-new chapter in my life. I just knew it somehow.

That was the beginning of a new chapter for me in the area of being a lifelong learner.

It was the start of a season in my life where I basically became a sponge, soaking up music like crazy. Jazz, folk, instrumental, rock, singer-songwriter, classical, and on and on. During that year after my graduation, I was still living at home. I started playing around on the upright piano that had been sitting in my parents' living room for years.

Let me tell you about this piano. My sweet parents bought it for $50 from a local church that was unloading several of them. I remember the day these two huge guys came and delivered it off the back of a truck. I was like eight years old at the time. My sister wanted to take piano lessons, and she begged and begged them to buy her one. So, they finally did it. Three weeks later she said, "I want to be a cheerleader!" So there the piano sat, for many a year. It became reduced to being the spot where my parents had put the stereo up on top, a few plants as well. My dad even took out the lower panel, and attached some brackets so it would store his rifles in there. For real!

After those years of sitting dormant, it now became my playground. Something inside of me had been ignited. The music was in my bones. For whatever reason, I could hear a song being played, and I could figure it out on the piano. I wasn't technically great, but things just clicked.

Once I started down that road, was I done learning? No way. It was just the beginning of learning. Now as I look back, what a journey. I've learned and experienced so much about everything from arrangement, melody, dynamics, recording, mixing—all that. I was blessed to be able to play music live for thousands of people. In some small way, it seemed I had some of it figured out. And at the same time, there's a feeling of not knowing anything at all. What makes a good song? If I'm honest, I have no idea.

This is kind of the mystery of desiring to be a lifelong learner.

As I spoke to so many people this year, it was a common theme that kept coming up—a desire to unearth more and keep learning. Also, FYI, my sister who had abandoned the idea of playing the piano later picked up guitar, and is now a full-time worship leader in Oklahoma. She told me not too long ago that she's picking up the piano again. She's a lifelong learner.

You have this desire, too. Maybe there's a certain area of life that just intrigues you, and you've always wished you could learn how to do it: flying a plane, playing an instrument, building a treehouse. Maybe there is something stirring inside you that longs to take you deeper within. Maybe there's a desire to know more scripture, be a better leader, or visit historical places. I'm telling you, there's something in us that spurs us on to be a lifelong learner. I also know there is a voice that tells us it's too much hassle, not to worry about it, or that it's not worth the effort.

I hope you find some inspiration in the next couple of interviews. I say, go for it. Go and learn and be a sponge. You never know where that road will take you.

Fun fact: Twenty-five or so years after my hearing that Grammy Award-winning Andreas Vollenweider album being played in the store, my wife gave me the most amazing birthday present ever. We flew to Virginia to see him and his band in a very intimate setting at Wolf Trap. He had not been to the US in over a decade, and we got to see him live in this old barn venue that seated like 450 people. Unreal.

Does this not show the deep love my wife has for me? To fly to another state to go see a harp guy. That's real love, I say. But I'll tell you what, that night I found myself mesmerized again. Hearing musicians who care so deeply about their work will do nothing short of inspire the heart. I even took note of the sound man. I noticed him working feverishly behind the console during the first couple songs, trying to help translate to the best of his ability the instruments to the room he was mixing for. He looked like a chef who was focused on putting just the right ingredients together. No, he looked like a glass blower who was running back and forth between heating up the fire and turning the glass so it would have the perfect color combination when it was finished. During the last song, I looked back at the sound guy again. Was he sitting back in his chair coasting to the end? Nope. He was standing over the audio console, tweaking knobs, making adjustments, caring about every detail. There's that meraki thing again.

That night we got to meet Andreas and his band afterward. I got to share my push broom experience in 1987, how I was stopped in my tracks. He was kind, probably thought I was a little weird. But I also suspect he knows exactly what I'm talking about.

His percussion guy, Andi Pupato, and I became friends that night. We've kept in touch over the years, and my wife and I even connected and had lunch with him in Switzerland several years ago. It's crazy how so many things really do connect and lead us back to relationships.

I get inspired by people who desire to never quit learning. Last year I was blessed to do the music at a memorial service for a sweet lady who had passed away at the age of ninety. During the eulogy, her son spoke about her life. He said she loved clogging. You know, clogging? The folk dance that's done in a group with hard shoes for a percussive effect. He said she was an avid dancer, and traveled with a team, and did events. What she loved most about it was the people, and the fun they had together. Then something he said blew my mind. She started to learn clogging when she was seventy-five. I stood in the back of the room thinking, *This lady was awesome*. At seventy-five-years-old, she wasn't done. There were things she wanted to do and experience. I want to be like her.

Be a lifelong learner. I think God delights in us when we have a heart of a lifelong learner, to remain teachable. You never *ever* know where it will take you. Maybe you'll build the treehouse of your dreams! Maybe a tree of hope will grow in your spirit as you let the roots go down deep in your heart. Maybe you'll learn a new instrument, start painting, make a new friend from around the world, or even take up clogging! I think that there's joy to be found in learning.

# DAVE BARNES

*"You know, I wish there was some way to jump into the future and ask the seventy-five-year-old me, hey, did I do it alright? Have I been balancing it all okay? Relationships, family, love, time. But in real life, you don't get to do that."*

Super fun day in Nashville when I got to meet up with Dave Barnes for coffee. For those of you who are Dave fans, you're hating me just a little right now. For those of you who aren't familiar with his name, he's a pretty phenomenal singer-songwriter. He has released ten albums so far and has won several awards. Most notably, he was nominated for a Grammy for the song, "God Gave Me You," recorded by Blake Shelton. Aside from all that, he's pretty much hilarious. If you've taken five minutes to scroll through his Instagram posts over the past months and years, you'll see that Dave should actually be on late night TV.

One of the reasons I wanted to connect with Dave is this "lifelong learner" thing I'm talking about. Here's a guy who has been in one mode creatively, and then is now switching a little bit and learning as he goes. For years he was in the mode of "Dave Barnes" the artist/musician. From a songwriter perspective, he was writing his own tunes, that he would be performing and using to connect with his fans. But recently, after "God Gave Me You" blew up on the country music scene, it has launched Dave into his next "learning" season. A season that finds him writing tunes not only with other songwriters in the industry, but with the target of other people recording them.

I hope you enjoy my Q&A time with Dave. Since he and I were sitting in a coffee shop, go ahead grab some coffee and join us.

**WAYNE:** This is super cool to get to hang out for a bit. Thanks for letting me pick your brain.

**DAVE:** This is super cool what you are doing, chatting with all these different folks. I can't imagine all the nuggets you're getting from people. Thanks for including me.

**WAYNE:** Tell me a little bit about where you are creatively right now. I know there's a new aspect of your songwriting career, writing tunes for other people.

**DAVE:** Yes. Right now I'm kind of living in the space between being an artist and doing the songwriting thing for other artists, if that makes any sense. I'm getting into a room with other songwriters, daily, weekly, and some are younger than me, some older. When I'm working with other creatives, and songwriters specifically, I have to have humility and the desire to say, "Hey, I want to learn from you! That thing you did with those chord changes was awesome; how did you do that? Why did you do that?"

**WAYNE:** For those who don't write and perform their own tunes, it might be hard to get their mind around. But it's such an intimate thing when you are putting your own heart and story out there for people to hear. You're bearing your soul, basically. Then I bet it's odd to change gears and be like, Okay this is a song about "xyz" and it's for "xyz" artist.

**DAVE:** Sometimes I get whiplash from going from creating, this certain way, on my own stuff, to working with a team where I'm not in charge of anything. Like everyone else, I have a certain way of approaching my own tunes, in my little space-cranking away. But it's a totally different ballgame when you are with a team, and the goal is to work together to make the song the best it can be. It's stretching me a ton.

**WAYNE:** So cool. What a blessing, man. It's great that you have had the career track of success with your own songs, sharing straight to your fans. And now, you not only get to keep doing that, but you get to be pushed into a new area of learning from these other songwriters.

**DAVE:** I'm so thankful. Being a songwriter for a living is the greatest job in the world. As long as I can keep finding a way to pull it off!

**WAYNE:** I notice that sometimes these slight changes in career (or huge ones, for that matter) sometimes come in midlife. Thoughts on that?

**DAVE:** There's a great book that came out called *Halftime.* It talks about some of this. Seems like something switches when you hit that forty-ish age. I know in the music world, for sure, you can't just output what you did before—songs, touring, albums. I know some guys who are holding on to what they did before, and that just doesn't work well. I'm forty-one now, and as far as my songwriting goes, I am trying to be totally honest with my music. Why try and be anything else? I want to write about where I am in life, with my family, kids, trusting God with my future, all of it.

One of Dave's tunes on his last record is a song called "Having Kids." Do yourself a favor and go give it a listen. It's hilarious and somehow heart-wrenching at the same time.

**WAYNE:** I heard you have a theory about that "heart" feeling, and how much space there actually is within a person for music.

**DAVE:** Yeah, I have this crazy theory that basically everyone has only so much "gig space" of memory for music in their heart. This is full of things that happened when they were young, say thirteen to twenty-eight or so. Songs that are attached to a heart memory take up 35 percent of the gig space right away. It's basically within this age when someone is growing, experiencing, learning, traveling, falling in love, getting a broken heart. Someone may say, "Oh, man I love that song from this artist," and it occupies the space in that "heart feeling" that is so dear. The same artist can release a new tune five to ten years later, and it may have no impact on that same person, because it doesn't match the heart feeling, if that makes any sense at all?

**WAYNE:** Totally. We have seen the music industry change before our eyes in only a ten-year period. CDs gave way to iTunes, which now gives way to streaming services. There's good and bad in it, I know. What are your thoughts?

**DAVE:** The whole thing has obviously changed. One really good thing about things like Spotify is this: Say there is someone who is younger, part of the next generation, and they stumble onto a playlist of someone else, and they might hear your song, where they never would have before. Now, all of a sudden, your music is being heard by someone that might totally connect with that heart feeling I was talking about. For example, when I see my kids start dancing around in our house to a certain song, and I see the complete and utter joy on their faces, all of a sudden, I'm like, boom—"heart drive."

**WAYNE**: Okay, one last question. What would forty-one-year-old Dave tell twenty-year-old Dave?

**DAVE**: I wish there was some way to jump into the future and ask the seventy-five-year-old me, "Hey, did I do it alright? Have I been balancing it all okay? Relationships, family, love, time." But in real life, you don't get to do that. It's really about having faith, I think, a matter of trust. I would say, "Don't freak out. Trust God with every area of your life."

# DAVID ARMS

*"I truly think the saddest place to be
is in a place where you are tired of learning."*

David Arms is a painter and author whose gallery space is based in Leiper's Fork, Tennessee, just outside of Nashville. His gallery is in an amazing old barn that seems to beckon you to sit and stay awhile. I met up with David there in Leiper's Fork in the rolling hills of Tennessee. When I say rolling, I mean rolling. This place is beautiful. If you are ever in the area, be sure to make it a stop.

He walked me around his place there, and then we took a seat inside the nearby Leiper's Creek Gallery. Lisa Fox, the owner there, brought us a tray of finger foods and drinks. They were so welcoming and fun, it was a treat. As we chatted, he and I found we actually had many things in common. He and his wife were ten years into their marriage before having kids, just like us. He and his wife did classical homeschooling, just like us. His family loves art and creating, very much like us. We jumped into faith and art, and he had so much to share.

**DAVID:** Congrats on being a dad of two little girls! Pray for your future sons-in-law. I did this very seriously over the years my daughter was growing up, and God really answered that one; he's my best friend now. Just a suggestion for you. And, also, it won't be who you expect!

**WAYNE:** Yes and yes! Tell me about your art, your craft, and how is it that you've been able to carve out such a successful career as an artist?

**DAVID:** I guess in one word, "authenticity." It lasts. Trends don't last, but be true to yourself, your calling and vision, and it will be fruitful. Be true to yourself. Why spend time and energy trying to be like someone else?

**WAYNE:** In terms of selling your art, where do you stand on the whole "I only sell originals" versus "I sell prints of my work" discussion. Some people are purists in this deal, and some are just thrilled to get their work out there. Your thoughts?

**DAVID**: That old saying, "I came for the have and for the have nots," I love the fact that I sell prints and cards of my work. It's about the joy of having my work be interacting with someone's life! I get just as much excitement from selling a $3 card as I do a $10,000 original painting.

> We chatted about this journey I have been on, connecting with so many people, and desiring to learn from them. I shared how encouraging and eye opening it's been for me. In many ways I'm being reminded that I want to be a lifelong learner.

**DAVID**: I truly think the saddest place to be is in a place where you are tired of learning. I can't imagine a life without creativity, walking closely with God, holding hands through this life. In terms of years, why would I want to go back? Every year is the best! I'm closer to the end! It's been an amazing ride and continues to get better.

As we wrapped up our time together, he was so generous. He gave me a copy of his beautiful new book that is full of his paintings and works. His words were still ringing in my heart as I drove back through the Tennessee hills. "I can't imagine a life without creativity, walking closely with God, holding hands through this life."

Beautiful.

> "My dad is ninety-six years old and said last week,
> 'My greatest days are still in front of me.'
> My dad will live until the day he dies."[18]
>
> —John Maxwell

## SOME THINGS TO KICK AROUND

1. Which of these interviews thus far has spoken to you the most?

_____

_____

_____

_____

2. Something I've always wanted to learn or pick up and try is:

_____

_____

_____

_____

3. Here is how I will apply "Lifelong Learner" to my life starting now:

_____

_____

_____

_____

## chapter nine
# GET TO KNOW THE STORYTELLER

"He went back to teaching by the sea. A crowd built up to such a great size that he had to get into an offshore boat, using the boat as a pulpit as the people pushed to the water's edge. He taught by using stories . . . many stories."

—Mark 4:1-2 (MSG)

Jesus was THE storyteller. He used story all the time. He met people where they were. Whether you are a person of faith or not, hang with me here. I think Jesus knows that there is a bigger story going on with all of us. Check out what Jesus had to say as He sat out on that boat. Can you just picture the scene with all those folks sitting quietly so they could hear His every word? It's recorded in Mark 4:

> "Listen. What do you make of this? A farmer planted seed. As he scattered the seed, some of it fell on the road and birds ate it. Some fell in the gravel; it sprouted quickly but didn't put down roots, so when the sun came up it withered just as quickly. Some fell in the weeds; as it came up, it was strangled among the weeds and nothing came of it. Some fell on good earth and came up with a flourish, producing a harvest exceeding his wildest dreams.
>
> "Are you listening to this? Really listening?" (vv 3–9, MSG)

When Jesus asks if we are listening, something within me wants to make sure I dial in my heart and attention. The story in Mark 4 continues:

> He continued, "Do you see how this story works? All my stories work this way.
>
> "The farmer plants the Word. Some people are like the seed that falls on the hardened soil of the road. No sooner do they hear the Word

than Satan snatches away what has been planted in them.

"And some are like the seed that lands in the gravel. When they first hear the Word, they respond with great enthusiasm. But there is such shallow soil of character that when the emotions wear off and some difficulty arrives, there is nothing to show for it.

"The seed cast in the weeds represents the ones who hear the kingdom news but are overwhelmed with worries about all the things they have to do and all the things they want to get. The stress strangles what they heard, and nothing comes of it.

"But the seed planted in the good earth represents those who hear the Word, embrace it, and produce a harvest beyond their wildest dreams." (vv 13–20, MSG)

As I am navigating the areas of my heart that are calling me to be brave, I really need to walk closely with THE storyteller. Jesus is still talking to us today, all the time! My next interview is with someone who has walked with Jesus a long time. Super inspiring. Buckle up.

## JOHN ELDREDGE

> "I walked out the coffee shop, and I had this old Jeep Wagoneer.
> In the old days you needed an actual key to get in the door.
> I put my key in the door, and I literally very clearly heard Jesus say,
> 'That was a really bad decision.' I was like, 'What!' I walked back into
> the coffee shop, he's still sitting there, and I said, 'Okay, I'm in.'"

John Eldredge is an author, counselor, and teacher who heads up Wild at Heart, a ministry designed to help people restore their hearts to God. He has literally sold millions of books, spoken around the world, and impacted many lives. But what I love the most about John is the unassuming way he speaks directly to readers' hearts. I had read his book *Wild at Heart* about ten years ago and loved it. Then it sat on my bookshelf for a while. I've appreciated other books from him, but that one still always sticks out to me.

About two years ago (as I shared earlier) I was doing some serious soul searching. It was actually at about the same time this book journey began. I was turning fifty, and I was about to be on sabbatical. But bigger than that, I was asking God some big questions about my work and calling.

I was weighing out heavily the major decision of whether to continue working full time in my church position or to step back slightly and pursue my art and other creative endeavors. As I mentioned earlier, my degree from years ago was in art, and my desire to use my art skills was making a strong resurgence in my heart. I was asking big questions about what I should be pursuing with my days. I was praying—a lot! I was trying to get advice from anyone who would give it.

Then one day I saw *Wild at Heart* sitting on my bookshelf. I thought, *Oh, I remember that book; I love it.* I opened it up to where I'd left a bookmark near a quote I'd liked reading by Howard Thurman. Here is was again, the quote that read: "Don't ask yourself what the world needs. Ask yourself what makes you come alive, and then go do that. Because what the world needs is people who have come alive."

Oh, no. I slammed the book shut. But the quote was good for me to read. God was at work in my heart. The storyteller was calling me deeper into the bigger story that we are all in.

That same year, I signed up for the Wild at Heart men's conference that you heard me talk about earlier. It was so great to be with 450 other guys who were asking most of the same questions as me, like, "Do I have what it takes?" and "God, are You in this?"

I knew once *Braving* starting coming together, I needed to interview John. I also knew that if I was going to talk deeply about this "storyteller" Jesus, I wanted to connect with John Eldredge.

I just had to find some creative way to convince him to grant me an interview.

I tried pretty much everything at my disposal, short of showing up at his Colorado office with my guitar. I did send him that "Brunch" painting I mentioned earlier. He had pity on me, I think, and thankfully agreed to chat. We connected via Zoom for an amazing interview. Super excited to share parts of it with you; his heart comes through big time.

**JOHN:** Pretty risky to send people art.

**WAYNE:** Ha-ha! Yes. That's probably right. I just thought, *Hey, this guy is using his art to connect to people, I'm doing the same thing.*

**JOHN:** It's awesome! Hey, before we get started, we have a puppy, and it sounds like the puppy has just gotten into something. Hold on one second!

Then he ran off. I sat there looking at an empty chair for a bit, and then realized, *Whoa, look at John's office!* There was a sword on the wall, tons of books on his shelves, and I thought to myself, *This is freaking incredible!* After a minute or two, John returned with two dogs who were playing and chewing on each other's ears, full of joy.

**WAYNE:** They're awesome! Nothing destroyed?

**JOHN:** Nothing that can't be destroyed.

**WAYNE:** Well, I am currently living the exact opposite of this scene. I have two little girls, five and seven, and they are amazing. As of like ten days ago, we now have a cat in our house.

**JOHN:** I'm so sorry.

**WAYNE:** I just don't get it—cats, I mean. We had a husky for twelve years, and another husky before him. Dogs, I understand. When we first got the cat—her name is "Ms. Piccolo," by the way—on her first night here she chewed through a curling iron cord that was plugged in! My wife said, "Wayne, check this out—she bit through the cord, and it was plugged in!" The cat survived, we found the plug, but we couldn't find the curling iron! Unreal.

**JOHN:** You're a good dad, Wayne. You're a good dad.

**WAYNE:** Okay, my first question for you. I would love to hear the story of how your life took the turn from you being "theatrical guy" to "counselor" to "author" to now, really, "mentor" to many, many people? I don't know all the history of the creative side of your personality. I tell you, though, when I listen to your audio books, or on a podcast, when you start sharing a famous quote, I can hear it in your voice how that theatrical part of you just comes alive!

**JOHN:** Yeah, I tried myself to connect those dots not too long ago. You look back on your journey and try to say, "Okay, where's the hand of God in that?" I had an undergraduate in theater, ran a live theater program in LA with my wife, and absolutely loved it. We loved our life in the theater. What I loved was finding stories that moved people's hearts and souls. It wasn't just entertainment. Robert McGee, a fairly famous script doctor said, "People don't go to movies just for entertainment, they go to see a story that helps them understand their own story." So, in our early theater days we were after meaning, and moving people. Then, to be honest, though, the theater almost took my marriage. It's long hours, weekends, late nights, it's your whole life. There is little room for anything else. So, I walked away. I let it go. I was fairly lost for a few years; I worked in D.C. in policy, and wow, I was dying.

At this point, John references that old powerful, familiar quote, always worth considering, that I had read just before deciding to pursue this interview.

There's a quote from Howard Thurman, "Don't ask yourself what the world needs. Ask yourself what makes you come alive, and then go do that. Because what the world needs is people who have come alive." I was successful there in D.C., but inside I was dying. A friend said to me, "When you go into a bookstore, do you go to the politics and policy section?"

**WAYNE:** Ha-ha, probably not, right?

**JOHN:** That was my reaction exactly, like, "Yeah, I hate that stuff!" He asked me what I'm reading, and I said stuff on the soul. I'm drawn to things like counseling, work on the soul, wholeheartedness. And he said, "Dude, you are in the wrong career." From there, I moved to Colorado, got a degree in counseling, and started a private practice. I was sitting in my office listening to people's stories, and I was like, *Wow, I was made for this.* I was made to help people understand their story. It's just like in the theater, a good director has to get to the essence of the character's story. So, I kind of went from one story world, to another story world.

Cool story. My mentor, Brent, and I were sitting in a coffee shop together, and he puts this idea on the table. He said we should write a book together on all these things we were learning from these people's lives. At that time, my wife and I had young kids, like five, three, and one, all boys. I am finishing grad school, and I'm working days and nights. He throws this idea out, and I'm like, "No way, impossible." I walked out the coffee shop, and I had this old Jeep Wagoneer. In the old days you needed an actual key to get in the door. I put my key in the door, and I literally very clearly heard Jesus say, "That was a really bad decision." I was like, "What!" I walked back into the coffee shop, he's still sitting there, and I said, "Okay, I'm in." So together we wrote *Sacred Romance*. And what I learned in that process is that I love it. I love writing. It brought back my theater, as I used to write as well as act. So I fell into writing, communicating about God's story, our story. It was so wonderful and powerful and such a fit. I actually ended up quitting my practice because it just took off. A lot of the things in the book *Wild at Heart* came from my sessions with people.

**WAYNE:** That's so amazing. It's almost like, seeing God really multiplying things. Instead of you and one person at a time coming to sit with you, there was more for you on a whole different level.

**JOHN:** There was a whole series of massive risk taking in all this. I'm sitting in my office as a therapist one night, doing marriage counseling. I'm listening to this couple, and all of a sudden, Jesus steps in again. It was kind of like the coffee shop thing. Jesus said, "John, you are speaking to two people. I want you to speak to a lot more." That was out of nowhere; that's all He said. Driving home that night, I asked, "What was that all about?" And here's what he says, "Quit your practice." There was no *Wild at Heart*, there was no Ransomed Heart Ministry. *Sacred Romance* had come out, but that was it. Literally, the same week my publisher calls and said the book was going well for a first-time author and asked if I'd like to write again. I said, "Yeah, I have a few ideas." That was how it got going. And seriously, therapy is a wonderful profession. I recommend everyone to go do it, but for me, I was on a different path.

So I quit my job. No insurance. No guaranteed income. And then Ransomed Heart took off.

**WAYNE:** I guess it would have been way easier to take the faith step after the other things had gone really well, *Wild at Heart* selling hundreds of thousands of copies and being translated into different languages. Then say, "Okay, maybe we'll step out comfortably." I guess it doesn't really work that way.

**JOHN:** Nope, it sure doesn't.

**WAYNE:** Okay, let me pick your brain on the subject of creativity. For me, something that I've been wrangling with for the past couple years is, as a person of faith, the art or music that I create, I want it to be God-glorifying. I want to bring my very best work. But I guess there's tension about whether something is Christian art. Did I put a tiny cross on the Bear painting? No. Or, if I'm doing music, should it only fit within the boundaries of what works within the church? I follow y'all's podcast, and I know you guys have talked about this being a tough time on the human heart. And yet, even now, people are still trying to create art, create music. The human soul is still creating art out there.

I'm just curious what your take is on all that, and I'm not even really sure what the question is! [*laughs*]

**JOHN:** Let's begin by separating it from career, because that's a separate question. Have you read Hans Rookmaaker's book, *Art Needs No Justification*?

**WAYNE:** No, but the title sounds awesome.

**JOHN:** Yeah, you would dig it. It was published in the 70s, I think. He was actually a famous Dutch art historian. I actually agree with him. Dostoevsky had a quote, "Beauty will save the world." Especially in times of cultural trauma, we need beauty more than ever. Beauty heals, beauty speaks, beauty declares that good will win in the end. I was just teaching this at a conference last weekend. You know, we need oxygen, so the world is saturated with oxygen. God arranged it so we have a renewable supply; it's really cool. We need water, so the world is saturated with water; we're the blue planet. The world is also saturated with beauty! God must have thought we need it like we need water and we need air. To me, the world is more beautiful than it is functional. That is a really big shift for someone raised in the Western world in the last 200 years. Because we have actually worshipped function and efficiency. Here you have something that is gloriously inefficient. In fact, George MacDonald's line is, "Gloriously wasteful, O my Lord, art thou!" He's talking about sunset after sunset, you just paint them and throw them away. So, beauty saturates the world, the human soul needs beauty. People will seek beauty, arrange for beauty. I think that's essential for what it means to be a human being. So does it need to have a cross on it, I don't think so. The sun doesn't have a cross on it, the moon doesn't have a cross on it. But, yes, the Psalms say that they speak, creation speaks.

Then, into creativity a little bit, this is fascinating. One of the things that really got my attention as a therapist was this—as people began to heal, they became creative.

**WAYNE:** Wow!

**JOHN:** And it wasn't just like one client, it wasn't two. I watched this phenomenon take place over dozens and dozens of lives. Different stories, different ages. I was really intrigued by this. As people heal, they become more playful, they become more loving. As people heal and become restored to who they are created to be, they become more creative. That is just fascinating to me. That must mean that in the coming Kingdom, there's just tons of creativity. Right? Because people are well and whole, and living in what we were made to live. I think creativity is essential for man to live. Paul says something really interesting—I can't remember exactly which letter it was in—but he's talking about the world spinning off its axis. He said, "Having lost all sensitivity, they have given themselves over to sensuality." I think as human beings experience healing, there's a sensitivity that returns, and that wants to be creative. There's a jillion ways it can be done. An elegant math equation can be beautiful. Surgery done well can be absolutely beautiful.

A moment ago I separated career out of it, because in this hour on the earth, where everything is so broken, very few people get to make a living from their gifting. Incredibly talented musicians are baristas, and immensely talented teachers are working at the mill. People have a very hard time reconciling their calling to their income. I would want to keep those things separate for a while. But . . . but, that doesn't mean you shouldn't pursue your calling! Right? We all gotta make a living, but you can't abandon your calling. There are a lot of people out there, artists, poets, who abandoned their calling because they couldn't make a living at it. And I'm like, *Whoa, whoa, time out.* Those things don't always harmonize in this world; I wish they did. There's many doctors who would love to quit their job tomorrow and write! We can't abandon our calling. We do it because it brings us joy. We do it because we can't imagine not doing it.

I think that God can help us navigate those tough questions into a place where we can flourish. I do. For me, I was basically in exile in Washington, D.C. I was dying. I was well paid. I was being promoted, but I was dying. I had to take a big risk. But this is what I firmly believe: If you will follow Jesus closely—not just say, "Tomorrow, I'm going to quit and go build boats." Then maybe, maybe in seven years that may happen. But man, stay close to God, that would be my counsel to people. You have to let Him shepherd you through this disaster called "the world" around us.

**WAYNE:** Okay, shifting gears just a little bit. How do you handle it when little darts come your way when you are trying something new? For example, even jumping into this book project, I heard the little voices of doubts within my own heart. Or realizing it very well may be the enemy who is trying to derail you. Or when other people say things off the cuff, or when they're trying to be funny. Last week, a guy literally said to me, "Hey, I see you're putting a book out. So you're a musician, an artist, and you're an author, now, too?" I walked away kind of like, *What was that?* Was that a side compliment, or a weird thing? Or even my own thoughts like, *Should I even mess with this; is anyone going to even care to read it?* I know I've heard you talk about "making agreements" with thoughts that may pop into your mind, or with what others say. Do you ever have those "discouragement" type things?

**JOHN:** Of course. Because art is opposed. Your calling is opposed. Beauty is opposed. Life is opposed. Of course. If you are not encountering opposition, you are probably not in the right place. I mean, right? Really. But you have to understand, some of those comments come out of envy. Envy is horrible, but our whole culture encourages it. People will envy your ability to create, the freedom to do it. Envy is horrible. These are the human nature things. Then you have the internal struggles of any person who is trying to do a good work in the world. You need to pay attention to that actually, in this regard. The Russian playwright Anton Chekhov said, "If you want to work on your art, work on your life."

**WAYNE:** Wow. Wow.

**JOHN:** Yeah, that's where I, as a therapist, want to say, "Yes! Amen! Deal with your junk!" Because that stuff presents itself in terms of doubt. Doubt of yourself, doubt of your work, doubt if you should continue—all that.

**WAYNE:** There's something below the surface probably.

**JOHN:** Exactly. That's the beautiful territory of Jesus. He loves to get in there and work with that stuff. So, rather than say something like, "Think positive thoughts," I would encourage you to ask yourself where that doubt is coming from, and invite Christ into it.

And then, that third category is the evil one and his hatred of humanity, his hatred of beauty, his hatred of anything that reflects the glory of God. He will come after you, and this is the agreements thing—"You suck at this. You're never going to make it"—all that. You gotta be careful not to make agreements in your heart with any of that. The beauty of all this is, in all three of these categories, Jesus gave us the simplest test. He said, "You will know them by their fruit." If I accept that thought, or that comment that person made, what will be the fruit of it? Will it be further creativity and joy?

**WAYNE:** On a practical note, how do you balance calling/dreams/goals kind of stuff with family and family time? Significance versus success? It's a weird tension that's always there. How do you suggest to people, "Yes, pursue these things, but none of it is more important than what's really important?"

**JOHN:** My answer would be, very carefully. I hear people say, "I just want to chase a dream," or "I want to open a B&B," or "we are going to pull our kids out of school and travel." It's so cavalier. Like, do you understand? First off, you are dealing with something incredibly precious in your heart: Your dream is very precious. Guard that sucker! You are leaving your wallet on the hood of your car the way you are treating this! You have to treat this with immense care. Here's the deal, everything in this world is set against the restoration of your humanity and the realization of your dreams.

Let me give you some absolute practicals. I wrote my first three books in the unfinished basement of our house, with a bare lightbulb over my head . . .

**WAYNE:** *[laughing uncontrollably]*

**JOHN:** . . . while my sons made incredible racket upstairs, and would come down and interrupt me on a regular basis. You've just got to go, "This is what I've got. I've got these thirty minutes, I've got this hour, and that's okay." Because if it's the thing you really want to do, you're going to do it. I think it really comes back to this, the more that we align with God, that He is our first love, and that He is the great treasure of our life, the more we align with God, the more balance our lives will take on. And for you, Wayne, balancing young kids, your marriage, finishing a painting, going then to work, all that, He's able to do that. But if you try and do that by yourself, it's gonna be a mess. In John 15, Jesus says, "Apart from me you can do nothing." Without the presence of God in your life, you're going to gut it out; it will end up being really hard.

George MacDonald, the Scottish poet, writer, and pastor I quoted before, and who I adore, he says, "There is a reality in which all things are easy and plain, oneness with the Lord of life." Our lives are meant to be in actual union with God. Because out of that union, wow, the resiliency, the creativity, the cunning, the perseverance, the brilliance comes. I could say things like, "Prioritize yourself," and all that, but what is far more helpful is to tell you that, first off, you have to take this very seriously; we're talking about your dreams. Secondly, human beings are meant to live out of a united life with God—if you will pursue that!

All kinds of practical things. When I sit down to write, I worship first. I turn worship music on, I kneel down here in my office, and I worship! I align with God; I come into union with Jesus. I don't just start banging away on the keyboard. That's a brutal way to write! Then, I invoke the creative life of God into my work. I pray that. I invoke Genesis 1, the creative rule of God into my work. Those two things as a practice, as a way of life, is completely different. You know, I have a life, I have kids, I have a mortgage, I don't just sit around and write all day. So, in those windows that I do have, I want to treat them with great care. And also with a kind of kindness toward oneself. You've got to be really careful of the kinds of expectations you put on yourself to produce. If you're not careful, you can damage your soul, discourage your heart, and pretty soon, you're not creating anymore.

**WAYNE:** One thing I wanted to share with you, about Boot Camp this last February. It was my first time to be a part of that deal, and it was during the "frozen tundra" week, where it was like a high of 3 degrees up in the Colorado mountains with 450 other guys. Amazing. I'm sure you hear quite a few stories of people having cool and powerful moments, and I wanted to share this with you. I will say, I don't often hear literally the voice of Jesus speak something to me, but the times I have, it's been so super clear! One of these times was while I was at the Boot Camp. After one of the sessions, we broke, and you said for everyone to go outside for like an hour of quiet time. You also said, "Nobody die out there, because it's like 2 degrees and snowing." I'm from Houston, and all of that seemed crazy to me. Thanks goodness I had at least one Patagonia jacket with me. So I walked out and headed in the direction of where this vista is looking out over the huge awe-inspiring valley. I started hiking that direction, and guys are all heading out on their own. There was a building right there to the left, that was basically under construction. A little cabin surrounded by chain link fence. And clear as a bell, God was like, "This is a good spot right here." I don't say this lightly, but the voice was unmistakable. So, I turned, and I thought, *This view kind of stinks*. If I can go up just a little farther—this is Colorado at it's very finest! Again, I felt like God said, "This is good; stop here." So, I look and there are piles of shingles with snow on them, boards stacked, new windows covered in snow. Basically, it looked like the construction had been put on pause for the season. I'm looking around a little confused. And literally, very clearly, Jesus said, "This is you."

**JOHN:** Yes!

**WAYNE:** I know! And I was like, "What!" Gosh, I'm going to start crying right now. I felt like he said, "I'm going to change out a wall here, and replace a window here . . ." But this is what was really sweet. He said, "I'm not going to do it for you, and I'm not going to ask you to do it by yourself, we can do it together." So, I'm standing there crying like a little kid in front of this random construction site. I just want you to know that those kinds of moments are happening in people's lives; it happened in mine.

What was also trippy was that later in my sabbatical, was an exchange I had with one of the guys I met with, Zach Neese, who is a worship leader at Gateway Church. While I was telling him this story, he goes, "Oh yeah. *Tekton.*" I said, "God bless you—wait, what?" He said, "*Tekton* is the Greek word for "carpenter," the profession of Jesus and Joseph, his father. Most of the time we think of woodworker, but a tekton is really more of a stone mason, a home-builder, in that part of the world. He said that most likely, Jesus was a pretty muscular guy with callused hands, as in this profession they would've worked cutting rock and building homes every day. Zach continued, "Pretty cool that the 'home builder' of the universe told you that he wants to work on your house." It was cool to know that he is not done with me yet."

**JOHN:** That's awesome!

**WAYNE:** I just wanted you to hear; I'm not too sure how often you get to hear these types of stories.

**JOHN:** Just a little joy. I feel like a *constant* renovation project. We are all under renovation.

**WAYNE:** Yes! Okay, I'm not alone. One last question, what would fifty-nine-year-old John tell twenty-one-year-old John?

**JOHN:** This is easy. This is what I wish an older man had said to me: "You're gonna be okay." I know that sounds simple. But so much of what the young guy, the young artist, the young dreamer does is done out of uncertainty. It's done out of fear; it's done to prove oneself. You know, all that cluster of stuff. There's a lot of chaos. And to have someone say, "You're going to be okay." And then the other thing I'd say to my younger self is, "Don't be discouraged that it takes time." Most really good things in life do, you know? Whether it's an eighteen-year-old scotch, or how long it takes to write a book, don't be discouraged by how long it takes. I think I had a set of expectations that things would unfold much more quickly than they did, that I'd get out of my day job quicker, all that. There's just a graciousness to say, *You're gonna be fine. And things are gonna take a little longer than you think they will, and that's okay, too.*

What a mind-blowing and encouraging time I had with John that day. When I grow up, I want to be like him. As I grow, I sure do want to walk closely with the Storyteller. I want to walk closely with Jesus. Then I think it'll be pretty easy to be brave.

# SOME THINGS TO KICK AROUND

1. What is something that really struck you within this chapter?

_____

_____

_____

_____

_____

_____

2. If you're honest, I mean brutally, sincerely honest, what do I really think about this whole "God" thing?

_____

_____

_____

_____

_____

_____

3. Do you think God speaks to people today? Or no way? Have you experienced this in your own life?

_____

_____

_____

_____

_____

_____

_____

4. Here is how I will apply "Get to Know the Storyteller" to my life starting now:

_____

_____

_____

_____

_____

_____

## conclusion (or beginning)
# GO. BE. BRAVE.

"You're braver than you believe, stronger than you seem, and smarter than you think."[19]

—Winnie the Pooh

Today I am back again, sitting up in my treehouse, and I'm thinking lots about *your* treehouse. I'm thinking about the unknown adventure you are about to embark upon. I'm beyond excited for you. I'm thinking about you maybe being like a wild mustang about to jump over the wall and head into amazing places—the likes of which you've never dreamed—and I'm excited for you. I'm thinking about you giving your best to your work, giving your meraki to your organization or craft. I'm through-the-roof pumped for you. I'm thinking of you longing to get to know the storyteller in a deeper and more authentic way, and this humbles my heart.

What a journey it has been.

I really want to thank you so much for taking the time and heart energy to read this book. I pray it's been a blessing in some way, and that it has inspired you to go be brave. Thank you, for real.

I've learned so much through the process of putting this book together, more than I can even describe. I've learned that time really does move quickly. When I started this book project, my fiftieth birthday was arriving, and now, in one week, I turn fifty-two. Wow! I'm marveling that it took right at two years to compile all of these interviews and get them down on paper, but I'm so glad I did. I have a whole new level of respect for authors out there, because seeing a book to its full completion is a major deal. For me, it took a while because my family comes first. Often, I'd sit down to type away, and I'd hear one of my girls calling for me, so back downstairs I'd go with only three sentences completed.

Ah, #Dadlife. But that's the way I like it. I don't do the best job every single day, but for me, my family is most important.

I am reminded and challenged to be a lifelong learner. There are new adventures to experience, and new journeys to share with those we love. There are new projects, moments, and memories to create. There are new opportunities to encourage and love others well.

I'm also marveling that this treehouse is still standing! Yes. So far, so good.

I'm reminded to be present in the moment, because we really do look up and the moment is gone. We should treasure each one.

Even though I am wrapping up the entries in this book, the process for all of us is really just beginning. Or rather, it is never ending, right? Each of us is a work in progress.

Let's keep this conversation going. I would love to invite you to continue this journey, and to hear your thoughts and of the adventures you are on. I've launched a website **www.bravingbook.com** and there you can find out more ways to keep this discussion going. Please drop me a note.

There will also be a *Braving* podcast up and running, where I will circle back around to some of these folks and share the interviews online with you, as well as connect with other amazing people. Keep an eye out for it.

As my fifty-first year is now coming to an end, I've been thinking about something: For the last couple years, as my birthday rolls near, I ask God a question. I ask, "God, do you have a word for me for this coming year? Something I can hang my hat on, work toward, or refine?"

When I was turning fifty, clear as day, it was "epic." And *epic* it was. My family and I had so many adventures, it was unreal. I also launched into this project and met all of these amazing people you've read about. Our family hiked Yosemite for days! It was beyond epic.

When I was turning fifty-one, clear as day, I heard in my heart the word "wonder."

This year has had plenty of ups and downs, including the pandemic. I changed my role at church and took a voluntary pay cut in order to pursue my art and music efforts. Over a six-month period, I had ten major events cancel. Many times during this year I found myself *"wonder"ing* what in the world was going on? But as the year rounded up for me, and as I now look back, I'm in awe and wonder of God's hand as a provider, restorer, and Father. It actually has been a year of WONDER.

So now here we are today, my fifty-second year is about to start. I've been praying and asking, without getting a clue. Well, finally today it came. If I'm honest, I shared with God that "braving" might be a great option, since, you know, I have a book coming out, and it's all about braving, etc. Guess what? God said, "Nope—the word for you this year is ABIDE." Jesus says, "Abide in me, and I will abide in you. You will bear fruit, fruit that will last" (John 15:4).

And guess what I realized? This is big: If I abide, I don't really have to worry about trying to be brave. Maybe I should have called this book *Abiding*.

Maybe you could ask God if there's a word for you? It might actually surprise you.

Okay, I have one last story to share with you all before we wrap this up. It was yet another huge moment that came from being out here on our property. Maybe it's just how I'm wired, but God keeps dropping amazing truths on me when I am out in creation and nature.

The back part of our property borders a creek bed. From the ground level, you have to climb down about twenty feet to get to the water's edge. Every single time we go out there, it looks so different.

We have seen the creek nearly completely dried up.

We have seen the creek flowing so clearly that you could see hundreds of fish.

We've seen it so still and murky that I'd swear nothing could survive in there.

We've seen it come raging up over the twenty-foot barrier and flood part of the property during a major storm.

I think you get the picture. You never know what to expect when you walk down there.

Truth be told, it's my wife's very favorite part about the entire place. She *loves* being down there, ankle-deep in water, walking around with the girls. Usually while this is happening, I am keeping all eyes peeled for any snakes or other unwelcome guests. (#Dadlife.)

We've had kids out there to visit with our girls and they build little dams and tiny villages.

One day, we went down there with a few friends, and the creek was totally still and the surface was covered with algae. It was eerily quiet. The normal sound of running water falling over the rocks was missing. There was no movement. No breeze. Nada.

Kelley was showing them around and then she started seeing some spots where some fallen leaves and limbs had gotten all bunched up. To help clear things up, they all started removing some debris a little at a time, when something super cool happened. A bit of movement started happening in the water. It was like a teeny tiny door had been opened up to allow for some of the water to pass through.

After three or four minutes, as more debris was being cleared, I started to hear the slight sound of water going over the rocks down at the other end. This water was starting to move.

I was standing about thirty feet away, near the deeper end, and I saw the surface of the water. I shouted, "Hey y'all, something's happening! I can see the water moving!" They all yelled back, "Woohoo!" and kept clearing, more aggressively now.

Within minutes, the waterfall started getting louder and louder. The movement in the deep end where I stood was really picking up speed. The gunk was moving out from the surface, and we could all see down into the creek itself. I could see down to the bottom. Now they were at an even more frenzied pace of clearing things out because this creek was coming back to life.

Meanwhile, a cool breeze flew in quick, as a storm was rolling in. "The rain is coming, guys; we better wrap this up!" I shouted at everyone.

This was a magical and special moment to witness. The next thing I knew, the creek had become a full-blown river. All of the hindrances and debris had been cleared, and it was moving again. The waterfall was now loud, almost as loud as all of the cheering from my wife and her friends (and my girls, as well). The temperature dropped 10 degrees cooler and instantly the rain began falling. All I could hear was shouts for joy and a mighty waterfall.

Just like that, I think we all felt it. God was showing us something.

My amazing wife Kelley commented on how this is so much like our spiritual lives. We get bogged down, and without really realizing it, we turn into something we were not created to be. Our hearts are created to be clear, beautiful, and raging streams. Not murky, stagnant places.

We have experienced this with Jesus in our lives. He is so good, and desires to come and take the gunk out of our river so that it may flow again.

How can I pursue a dream in this life if my heart has grown murky? If my heart is like a river, then I want it flowing freely. These verses came to mind, and I'd love to share with you:

> "Whoever believes in me, as Scripture has said, rivers of living water will flow from within them" (John 7:38, NIV).

> "Do not conform to the pattern of this world, but be transformed by the renewing of your mind. Then you will be able to test and approve what God's will is—his good, pleasing and perfect will" (Romans 12:2, NIV).

> "Behold, I am doing a new thing; now it springs forth, do you not perceive it? I will make a way in the wilderness and rivers in the desert" (Isaiah 43:19, ESV).

You are in the midst of an epic story. You have one life to live, and the powerful thing is, the storyteller wants to walk with you on your adventure. Are you about to jump into your treehouse adventure? Don't let anything bog you down. Clear out the debris in your heart. Walk closely with God, abide in Him, and buckle up. It will be the ride of a lifetime. And you know what? That dream you have is there for a reason. You can do it!

I can't wait to see what happens.

# GO. BE. BRAVE.

*our Treehouse*

# WHAT TREEHOUSE ARE YOU BUILDING?

# about the author

Wayne Kerr is a creative, musician, songwriter, and visual artist based in Katy, Texas. Wayne has released 10 full-length albums and toured both nationally and internationally. He is also an award-winning painter and illustrator. Wayne had an original piece on display at the United Nations while in college. His artwork can be seen at juried art shows around the country several times per year. Wayne also currently serves part time as the Worship Leader for Grace Fellowship Church, a large mission-oriented congregation in Katy, Texas.

Wayne and his wife Kelley are currently living the BRAVING life daily, and enjoy watching and investing in their two girls every day. And unfortunately, the cat is still in his house, too.

For more information on Wayne's music,
please visit **www.waynekerrmusic.com**

For information on his art,
please see **www.kerrvillegallery.com**

To keep the conversation going with BRAVING,
please visit **www.bravingbook.com**

For more visit

# BRAVINGBOOK.COM

## "ROUND TOP CHAPEL"

FROM $75.00

DETAILS

SELECT DETAILS ▾

QUANTITY

1

ADD TO CART

f  ✦  in  ⌁

# KERRVILLEGALLERY.COM
*To see Waynes art*

Home    Bio    Schedule    Gallery    Tunes    + Follow    Contact

# WAYNEKERRMUSIC.COM
*For music links and updates*

# contact info page

We wanted you to have some compiled info on the amazing folks I interviewed for this project. Please check out their sites and follow their adventures. These artists, musicians, entrepreneurs, athletes, faith leaders, and more are being BRAVE out there. Keep up with them, and keep being inspired.

### DAVE BARNES
www.davebarnes.com | Instagram: @davebarnesmusic

### DAVID ARMS
Davidarms.com | Instagram: @davidarms.art.style.living

### NOAH ELIAS
www.noahelias.net | www.noahfineart.com | Instagram: @noah.j.elias

### ALBERT HANDELL
www.alberthandell.com

### MARK MAGGIORI
www.markmaggiori.com | Instagram: @markmaggiori

### JOHN ELDREDGE
www.wildatheart.org | Instagram: @ransomedheart

### TARA ROYER STEELE
www.royerspiehaven.com | Instagram: @tararoyersteele

### AINSLIE GROSSER
www.ainsliegrosser.com | Instagram: @ainsliegrosser

### FERNANDO ORTEGA
www.fernandoortega.com | Instagram: @phernandeau

### RAYMOND TURNER
www.mastermindartists.com

### JOHNNY CARRABBA
www.carrabbas.com | Instagram: @carrabbas

## MARK HARRIS
www.gatewaypeople.com | Instagram: @markharrismusic
Twitter: @markharrismusic

## DEBBIE BROWNE
www.leapingbutterfly.org | Instagram: @leapingbutterflyministry

## JUSTIN GERARD
www.gallerygerard.com | Instagram: @justingerardillustration

## CAM BECKMAN
www.pgatour.com

## ASHLEY FERGUSON
www.roundtop-marburgerfarm.com | Instagram: @marburgerfarm

## BEN CHAI
www.streetlightcadence.com | Instagram: @streetlightcadence

## MARY AND CRAIG JUTILA
www.whowillyouempower.com/maryjutila

## DAVID McCLISTER
www.davidmcclister.com | Instagram: @davidmcclisterphotography

## BEN MASTERS (FIN & FUR FILMS)
www.benmasters.com | Instagram: @bencmasters

## BEAU & KELLY BROTHERTON
www.bettertogetherlife.com | Instagram: @bettertogetherlife

## BRANDI LISENBE
www.doordyetx.com | Instagram: @doordyetx

## CONNOR KETCHUM
www.iliamnariverlodge.com | Instagram: @gotta_ketch_um_all

# endnotes

1. Eldredge, John, *Walking with God: How to Hear His Voice* (Nashville: Thomas Nelson, 2008).

2. Peter Jackson, director, *The Hobbit: An Unexpected Journey*, Metro-Goldwyn-Mayer (MGM), 2012.

3. P.J. Hogan, director, *Peter Pan*, Universal Pictures, 2003.

4. "Braving," dictionary.com. http://www.dictionary.com/browse/braving.

5. "Why Fingerprint Identification," The History of Fingerprints, onin.com, last updated September 29, 2020. https://onin.com/fp/fphistory.html.

6. Ada Mcvean, "Koalas have fingerprints just like humans," McGill, July 19, 2019. https://www.mcgill.ca/oss/article/did-you-know/koalas-have-fingerprints-just-humans.

7. J.R.R. Tolkien, *The Hobbit*, (London: George Allen & Unwin, 1937).

8. Ryan Dezember, "U.S. Oil Costs Less than Zero After a Sharp Monday Selloff," *Wall Street Journal*, last updated April 21, 2020. https://www.wsj.com/articles/why-oil-is-11-a-barrel-now-but-three-times-that-in-autumn-11587392745.

9. John C. Maxwell, "Increasing Your Vision," Global Leadership Network, accessed October 11, 2020. https://globalleadership.org/grow/growthtracks/john-maxwell-increasing-your-vision-1/?locale=en.

10. "The Harvard MBA Business School Study on Goal Setting," Wanderlust Worker, accessed October 11, 2020. https://www.wanderlustworker.com/the-harvard-mba-business-school-study-on-goal-setting/.

11. "Pelé quotes," Goodreads. https://www.goodreads.com/author/quotes/302745.Pel_.

12. "Meraki—Greek Word of the day—Doing it with love, passion and a lot of soul," Untranslatable Greek Words, Greeker Than The Greeks, accessed October 11, 2020. https://greekerthanthegreeks.com/2015/03/lost-in-translation-word-of-day-meraki.html.

13. "Georgia O'Keefe quotes," Goodreads. https://www.goodreads.com/author/quotes/140943.Georgia_O_Keeffe.

14. "Band History," Toto: 40 Trips Around the Sun. http://totoofficial.com/history/.

15. Richard Evans, quoting Carl W. Buehner, *Richard Evans' Quote Book*, (Indiana: Publishers Press, 1973).

16. Morgan Snyder, "What Is Your Epitaph?", Become Good Soil, accessed October 11, 2020. https://www.becomegoodsoil.com/2019/02/04/an-epitaph/.

17. "Walt Disney quote," Brainyquote. https://www.brainyquote.com/quotes/walt_disney_132637.

18. John C. Maxwell, "Increasing Your Vision," Global Leadership Network, accessed October 11, 2020. https://globalleadership.org/grow/growthtracks/john-maxwell-increasing-your-vision-1/?locale=en.

19. Carl Geurs, director, *Pooh's Grand Adventure: The Search for Christopher Robin*, Disney Television Animation, 1997.

Made in the USA
Middletown, DE
18 May 2021